The Principles of Success in Literature

The Principles of Success in Literature

George Henry Lewes

DD BOOKS
Publishers for New Generations

The Principles of Success in Literature
by George Henry Lewes

Price: ₹ 250/-

ISBN: 9789359576435

DD Books
Delhi, India

www.ddbookshub.com
ddsalesglobal@gmail.com

Printed in the **Republic of INDIA**

Table of Content

Chapter 1

I.

In the development of the great series of animal organisms, the Nervous System assumes more and more of an imperial character. The rank held by any animal is determined by this character, and not at all by its bulk, its strength, or even its utility. In like manner, in the development of the social organism, as the life of nations becomes more complex, Thought assumes a more imperial character; and Literature, in its widest sense, becomes a delicate index of social evolution. Barbarous societies show only the germs of literary life. But advancing civilisation, bringing with it increased conquest over material agencies, disengages the mind from the pressure of immediate wants, and the loosened energy finds in leisure both the demand and the means of a new activity: the demand, because long unoccupied hours have to be rescued from the weariness of inaction; the means, because this call upon the energies nourishes a greater ambition and furnishes a wider arena.

Literature is at once the cause and the effect of social progress. It deepens our natural sensibilities, and strengthens by exercise our intellectual capacities. It stores up the accumulated experience of the race, connecting Past and Present into a conscious unity; and with this store it feeds successive generations, to be fed in turn by them. As its importance emerges into more general recognition, it necessarily draws after it a larger crowd of servitors, filling noble minds with a noble ambition.

There is no need in our day to be dithyrambic on the glory of Literature. Books have become our dearest companions, yielding exquisite delights and inspiring lofty aims. They are our silent instructors, our solace in sorrow, our relief in weariness. With what enjoyment we linger over the pages of some well-loved author! With what gratitude we regard every honest book! Friendships, prefound and generous, are formed with men long dead, and with men whom we may never see. The lives of these men have a quite personal interest for us. Their homes become as consecrated shrines. Their little ways and familiar phrases become endeared to us, like the little ways and phrases of our wives and children.

It is natural that numbers who have once been thrilled with this delight should in turn aspire to the privilege of exciting it. Success in Literature has thus become not only the ambition of the highest minds, it has also become the ambition of minds intensely occupied with other means of influencing their fellow—with statesmen, warriors, and rulers. Prime ministers and emperors have striven for distinction as poets, scholars, critics, and historians. Unsatisfied with the powers and privileges of rank, wealth, and their conspicuous position in the eyes of men, they have longed also for the nobler privilege of exercising a generous sway over the minds and hearts of readers. To gain this they have stolen hours from the pressure of affairs, and disregarded the allurements of luxurious ease, labouring steadfastly, hoping eagerly. Nor have they mistaken the value of the reward. Success in Literature is, in truth, the blue ribbon of nobility.

There is another aspect presented by Literature. It has become a profession; to many a serious and elevating profession; to many more a mere trade, having miserable trade-aims and trade-tricks. As in every other profession, the ranks are thronged with incompetent aspirants, without seriousness of aim, without the faculties demanded by their work. They are led to waste powers which in other directions might have done honest service, because they have failed to discriminate between aspiration and inspiration, between the desire for greatness and the consciousness of power. Still lower in the ranks are those who follow Literature simply because they see no other opening for their incompetence; just as forlorn widows and ignorant old maids thrown suddenly on their own resources open a school—no other means of livelihood seeming to be within their reach. Lowest of all are those whose esurient vanity, acting on a frivolous levity of mind, urges them to make Literature a plaything for display. To write for a livelihood, even on a complete misapprehension of our powers, is at least a respectable impulse. To play at Literature is altogether inexcusable: the motive is vanity, the object notoriety, the end contempt.

I propose to treat of the Principles of Success in Literature, in the belief that if a clear recognition of the principles which underlie all successful writing could once be gained, it would be no inconsiderable help to many a young and thoughtful mind. Is it necessary to guard against a misconception of my object, and to explain that I hope to furnish nothing more than help and encouragement? There is help to be gained from a clear understanding of the conditions of success; and encouragement to be gained from a reliance on the ultimate victory of true principles. More than this can hardly be expected from me, even on the supposition that I have ascertained the real conditions. No one, it is to be presumed, will imagine that I can have any pretension of giving recipes for Literature, or of furnishing power and talent where nature has withheld them. I must assume the presence of the talent, and then assign the conditions under which that talent can alone achieve real success, no man is made a discoverer by learning the principles of scientific Method; but only by those principles can discoveries be made; and if he has consciously mastered them, he will find them directing his researches and saving him from an immensity of fruitless labour. It is something in the nature of the Method of Literature that I propose to expound. Success is not an accident. All Literature is founded upon psychological laws, and involves principles which are true for all peoples and for all times. These principles we are to consider here.

II.

The rarity of good books in every department, and the enormous quantity of imperfect, insincere books, has been the lament of all times. The complaint being as old as Literature itself, we may dismiss without notice all the accusations which throw the burden on systems of education, conditions of society, cheap books, levity and superficialty of readers, and analogous causes. None of these can be a VERA CAUSA; though each may have had its special influence in determining the production of some imperfect works. The main cause I take to be that indicated in Goethe's aphorism: "In this world there are so few voices and so many echoes." Books are generally more deficient in sincerity than in cleverness. Talent, as will become apparent in the course of our inquiry, holds a very subordinate position in Literature to that usually assigned to it. Indeed, a cursory inspection of the Literature of our day will detect an abundance of remarkable talent—-that is, of intellectual agility, apprehensiveness, wit, fancy, and power of expression which is nevertheless impotent to rescue "clever writing" from neglect or contempt. It is unreal splendour; for the most part mere intellectual fireworks. In Life, as in Literature, our admiration for mere cleverness has a touch of contempt in it, and is very unlike the respect paid to character. And justly so. No talent can be supremely effective unless it act in close alliance with certain moral qualities. (What these qualities are will be specified hereafter.)

Another cause, intimately allied with the absence of moral guidance just alluded to, is MISDIRECTION of talent. Valuable energy is wasted by being misdirected. Men are constantly attempting, without special aptitude, work for which special aptitude is indispensable.

"On peut etre honnete hornme et faire mal des vers."

A man may be variously accomplished, and yet be a feeble poet. He may be a real poet, yet a feeble dramatist, he may have dramatic faculty, yet be a feeble novelist. He may be a good story-teller, yet a shallow thinker and a slip-shod writer. For success in any special kind of work it is obvious that a special talent is requisite; but obvious as this seems, when stated as a general proposition, it rarely serves to check a mistaken presumption. There are many writers endowed with a certain susceptibility to the graces and refinements of Literature which has been fostered by culture till they have mistaken it for native power; and these men, being really destitute of native power, are forced to imitate what others have created. They can understand how a man may have musical sensibility and yet not be a good singer; but they fail to understand, at least in their own case, how a man may have literary sensibility, yet not be a good story-teller or an effective dramatist. They imagine that if they are cultivated and clever, can write what is delusively called a "brilliant style," and are familiar with the masterpieces of Literature, they must be more competent to succeed in fiction or the drama than a duller man, with a plainer style and slenderer acquaintance with the "best models." Had they distinctly conceived the real aims of Literature this mistake would often have been avoided. A recognition of the aims would have pressed on their attention a more distinct appreciation of the requirements.

No one ever doubted that special aptitudes were required for music, mathematics, drawing, or for wit; but other aptitudes not less special are seldom recognised. It is with authors as with actors: mere delight in the art deludes them into the belief that they could be artists. There are born actors, as there are born authors. To an observant eye such men reveal their native endowments. Even in conversation they spontaneously throw themselves into the characters they speak of. They mimic, often quite unconsciously the speech and gesture of the person. They dramatise when they narrate. Other men with little of this faculty, but with only so much of it as will enable them to imitate the tones and gestures of some admired actor, are misled by their vanity into the belief that they also are actors, that they also could move an audience as their original moves it.

In Literature we see a few original writers, and a crowd of imitators: men of special aptitudes, and men who mistake their power of repeating with slight variation what others have done, for a power of creating anew. The imitator sees that it is easy to do that which has already been done. He intends to improve on it; to add from his own stores something which the originator could not give; to lend it the lustre of a richer mind; to make this situation more impressive, and that character more natural. He is vividly impressed with the imperfections of the original. And it is a perpetual puzzle to him why the public, which applauds his imperfect predecessor, stupidly fails to recognise his own obvious improvements.

It is from such men that the cry goes forth about neglected genius and public caprice. In secret they despise many a distinguished writer, and privately, if not publicly, assert themselves as immeasurably superior. The success of a Dumas is to them a puzzle and an irritation. They do not understand that a man becomes distinguished in virtue of some special talent properly directed; and that their obscurity is due either to the absence of a special talent, or to its misdirection. They may probably be superior to Dumas in general culture, or various ability; it is in particular ability that they are his inferiors. They may be conscious of wider knowledge, a more exquisite sensibility, and a finer taste more finely cultivated; yet they have failed to produce any impression on the public in a direction where the despised favourite has produced a strong impression. They are thus thrown upon the alternative of supposing that he has had "the luck" denied to them, or that the public taste is degraded and prefers trash. Both opinions are serious mistakes. Both injure the mind that harbours them.

In how far is success a test of merit? Rigorously considered it is an absolute test. Nor is such a conclusion shaken by the undeniable fact that temporary applause is often secured by works which have no lasting value. For we must always ask, What is the nature of the applause, and from what circles does it rise? A work which appears at a particular juncture, and suits the fleeting wants of the hour, flattering the passions of the hour, may make a loud noise, and bring its author into strong relief. This is not luck, but a certain fitness between the author's mind and the public needs. He who first seizes the occasion, may be for general purposes intrinsically a feebler man than many who stand listless or hesitating till the moment be passed; but in Literature, as in Life, a sudden promptitude outrivals vacillating power.

Generally speaking, however, this promptitude has but rare occasions for achieving success. We may lay it down as a rule that no work ever succeeded, even for a day, but it deserved that success; no work ever failed but under conditions which made failure inevltable. This will seem hard to men who feel that in their case neglect arises from prejudice or stupidity. Yet it is true even in extreme cases; true even when the work once neglected has since been acknowleged superior to the works which for a time eclipsed it. Success, temporary or enduring, is the measure of the relatlon, temporary or enduring, which exists between a work and the public mind. The millet seed may be intrinsically less valuable than a pearl; but the hungry cock wisely neglected the pearl, because pearls could not, and millet seeds could, appease his hunger. Who shall say how much of the subsequent success of a once neglected work is due to the preparation of the public mind through the works which for a time eclipsed it?

Let us look candidly at this matter. It interests us all; for we have all more or less to contend against public misconception, no less than against our own defects. The object of Literature is to instruct, to animate, or to amuse. Any book which does one of these things succeeds; any book which does none of these things fails. Failure is the indication of an inability to perform what was attempted: the aim was misdirected, or the arm was too weak: in either case the mark has not been hit.

"The public taste is degraded." Perhaps so; and perhaps not. But in granting a want of due preparation in the public, we only grant that the author has missed his aim. A reader cannot be expected to be interested in ideas which are not presented intelligibly to him, nor delighted by art which does not touch him; and for the writer to imply that he furnishes arguments, but does not pretend to furnish brains to understand the arguments, is arrogance. What Goethe says about the most legible handwriting being illegible in the twilight, is doubtless true; and should be oftener borne in mind by frivolous objectors, who declare they do not understand this or do not admire that, as if their want of taste and understanding were rather creditable than otherwise, and were decisive proofs of an author's insignificance. But this reproof, which is telling against individuals, has no justice as against the public. For—and this is generally lost sight of—the public is composed of the class or classes directly addressed by any work, and not of the heterogeneous mass of readers. Mathematicians do not write for the circulating library. Science is not addressed to poets. Philosophy is meant for students, not for idle readers. If the members of a class do not understand—if those directly addressed fail to listen, or listening, fail to recognise a power in the voice—surely the fault lies with the speaker, who, having attempted to secure their attention and enlighten their understandings, has failed in the attempt? The mathematician who is without value to mathematicians, the thinker who is obscure or meaningless to thinkers, the dramatist who fails to move the pit, may be wise, may be eminent, but as an author he has failed. He attempted to make his wisdom and his power operate on the minds of others. He has missed his mark. MARGARITAS ANTE PORCOS! is the soothing maxim of a disappointed self-love. But we, who look on, may sometimes doubt whether they WERE pearls thus ineffectually thrown; and always doubt the judiciousness of strewing pearls before swine. The prosperity of a book lies in the minds of readers. Public knowledge and public taste fluctuate; and there come times when works which were once capable of instructing and delighting thousands lose their power, and works, before neglected, emerge into renown. A small minority to whom these works appealed has gradually become a large minority, and in the evolution of opinion will perhaps become the majority. No man can pretend to say that the work neglected today will not be a household word tomorrow; or that the pride and glory of our age will not be covered with cobwebs on the bookshelves of our children. Those works alone can have enduring success which successfully appeal to what is permanent in human nature—which, while suiting the taste of the day, contain truths and beauty deeper than the opinions and tastes of the day; but even temperary success implies a certain temporary fitness. In Homer, Sophocles, Dante, Shakspeare, Cervantes, we are made aware of much that no longer accords with the wisdom or the taste of our day—temporary and immature expressions of fluctuating opinions—but we are also aware of much that is both true and noble now, and will be so for ever.

It is only posterity that can decide whether the success or failure shall be enduring; for it is only posterity that can reveal whether the relation now existing between the work and the public mind is or is not liable to fluctuation. Yet no man really writes for posterity; no man ought to do so.

"Wer machte denn der Mitwelt Spass?"

("Who is to amuse the present?") asks the wise Merry Andrew in FAUST. We must leave posterity to choose its own idols. There is, however, this chance in favour of any work which has once achieved success, that what has pleased one generation may please another, because it may be based upon a truth or beauty which cannot die; and there is this chance against any work which has once failed, that its unfitness may be owing to some falsehood or imperfection which cannot live.

III.

In urging all writers to be steadfast in reliance on the ultimate victory of excellence, we should no less strenuously urge upon them to beware of the intemperate arrogance which attributes failure to a degraded condition of the public mind. The instinct which leads the world to worship success is not dangerous. The book which succeeds accomplishes its aim. The book which fails may have many excellencies, but they must have been misdirected. Let us, however, understand what is meant by failure. From want of a clear recognition of this meaning, many a serious writer has been made bitter by the reflection that shallow, feeble works have found large audiences, whereas his own work has not paid the printing expenses. He forgets that the readers who found instruction and amusement in the shallow books could have found none in his book, because he had not the art of making his ideas intelligible and attractive to them, or had not duly considered what food was assimilable by their minds. It is idle to write in hieroglyphics for the mass when only priests can read the sacred symbols.

No one, it is hoped, will suppose that by what is here said I countenance the notion which is held by some authors—a notion implying either arrogant self-sufficiency or mercenary servility—that to succeed, a man should write down to the public. Quite the reverse. To succeed, a man should write up to his ideal. He should do his very best; certain that the very best will still fall short of what the public can appreciate. He will only degrade his own mind by putting forth works avowedly of inferior quality; and will find himself greatly surpassed by writers whose inferior workmanship has nevertheless the indefinable aspect of being the best they can produce. The man of common mind is more directly in sympathy with the vulgar public, and can speak to it more intelligibly, than any one who is condescending to it. If you feel yourself to be above the mass, speak so as to raise the mass to the height of your argument. It may be that the interval is too great. It may be that the nature of your arguments is such as to demand from the audience an intellectual preparation, and a habit of concentrated continuity of thought, which cannot be expected from a miscellaneous assembly. The scholarship of a Scaliger or the philosophy of a

Kant will obviously require an audience of scholars and philosophers. And in cases where the nature of the work limits the class of readers, no man should complain if the readers he does not address pass him by to follow another. He will not allure these by writing down to them; or if he allure them, he will lose those who properly constitute his real audience.

A writer misdirects his talent if he lowers his standard of excellence. Whatever he can do best let him do that, certain of reward in proportion to his excellence. The reward is not always measurable by the number of copies sold; that simply measures the extent of his public. It may prove that he has stirred the hearts and enlightened the minds of many. It may also prove, as Johnson says, "that his nonsense suits their nonsense." The real reward of Literature is in the sympathy of congenial minds, and is precious in proportion to the elevation of those minds, and the gravity with which such sympathy moves: the admiration of a mathematician for the MECANIQUE CELESTE, for example, is altogether higher in kind than the admiration of a novel reader for the last "delightful story." And what should we think of Laplace if he were made bitter by the wider popularity of Dumas? Would he forfeit the admiration of one philosopher for that of a thousand novel readers?

To ask this question is to answer it; yet daily experience tells us that not only in lowering his standard, but in running after a popularity incompatible with the nature of his talent, does many a writer forfeit his chance of success. The novel and the drama, by reason of their commanding influence over a large audience, often seduce writers to forsake the path on which they could labour with some success, but on which they know that only a very small audience can be found; as if it were quantity more than quality, noise rather than appreciation, which their mistaken desires sought. Unhappily for them, they lose the substance, and only snap at the shadow. The audience may be large, but it will not listen to them. The novel may be more popular and more lucrative, when successful, than the history or the essay; but to make it popular and lucrative the writer needs a special talent, and this, as was before hinted, seems frequently forgotten by those who take to novel writing. Nay, it is often forgotten by the critics; they being, in general, men without the special talent themselves, set no great value on it. They imagine that Invention may be replaced by culture, and that clever "writing" will do duty for dramatic power. They applaud the "drawing" of a character, which drawing turns out on inspection to be little more than an epigrammatic enumeration of particularities, the character thus "drawn" losing all individuality as soon as speech and action are called upon. Indeed, there are two mistakes very common among reviewers: one is the overvaluation of what is usually considered as literary ability ("brilliant writing" it is called; "literary tinsel" would be more descriptive) to the prejudice of Invention and Individuality; the other is the overvaluation of what they call "solid acquirements," which really mean no more than an acquaintance with the classics. As a fact, literary ability and solid acquirements are to be had in abundance; invention, humour, and originality are excessively rare. It may be a painful reflection to those who, having had a great deal of money spent on their education, and having given a great deal of time to their solid aquirements, now see genius and original power of all kinds more esteemed than their learning; but they should reflect that what is learning now is only the diffused form of what was once invention. "Solid acquirement" is the genius of wits become the wisdom of reviewers.

IV.

Authors are styled an irritable race, and justly, if the epithet be understood in its physiological rather than its moral sense.

This irritability, which responds to the slightest stimulus, leads to much of the misdirection of talent we have been considering. The greatness of an author consists in having a mind extremely irritable, and at the same time steadfastly imperial:—irritable that no stimulus may be inoperative, even in its most evanescent solicitations; imperial, that no solicitation may divert him from his deliberately chosen aims. A magisterial subjection of all dispersive influences, a concentration of the mind upon the thing that has to be done, and a proud renunciation of all means of effect which do not spontaneously connect themselves with it—these are the rare qualities which mark out the man of genius. In men of lesser calibre the mind is more constantly open to determination from extrinsic influences. Their movement is not self-determined, self-sustained. In men of still smaller calibre the mind is entirely determined by extrinsic influences. They are prompted to write poems by no musical instinct, but simply because great poems have enchanted the world. They resolve to write novels upon the vulgarest provocations: they see novels bringing money and fame; they think there is no difficulty in the art. The novel will afford them an opportunity of bringing in a variety of scattered details; scraps of knowledge too scanty for an essay, and scraps of experience too meagre for independent publication. Others, again, attempt histories, or works of popular philosophy and science; not because they have any special stores of knowledge, or because any striking novelty of conception urges them to use up old material in a new shape, but simply because they have just been reading with interest some work of history or science, and are impatient to impart to others the knowledge they have just acquired for themselves. Generally it may be remarked that the pride which follows the sudden emancipation of the mind from ignorance of any subject, is accompanied by a feeling that all the world must be in the state of darkness from which we have ourselves emerged. It is the knowledge learned yesterday which is most freely imparted today.

We need not insist on the obvious fact of there being more irritability than mastery, more imitation than creation, more echoes than voices in the world of Literature. Good writers are of necessity rare. But the ranks would be less crowded with incompetent writers if men of real ability were not so often misdirected in their aims. My object is to decree, if possible, the Principles of Success—not to supply recipes for absent power, but to expound the laws through which power is efficient, and to explain the causes which determine success in exact proportion to the native power on the one hand, and to the state of public opinion on the other.

The laws of Literature may be grouped under three heads. Perhaps we might say they are three forms of one principle. They are founded on our threefold nature—intellectual, moral, and aesthetic.

The intellectual form is the PRINCIPLE OF VISION.

The moral form is the PRINCIPLE OF SINCERITY.

The aesthetic form is the PRINCIPLE OF BEAUTY.

It will be my endeavour to give definite significance, in succeeding chapters, to these expressions, which, standing unexplained and unillustrated, probably convey very little meaning. We shall then see that every work, no matter what its subject-matter, necessarily involves these three principles in varying degrees; and that its success is always strictly in accordance with its conformity to the guidance of these principles.

Unless a writer has what, for the sake of brevity, I have called Vision, enabling him to see clearly the facts or ideas, the objects or relations, which he places before us for our own instruction, his work must obviously be defective. He must see clearly if we are to see clearly. Unless a writer has Sincerity, urging him to place before us what he sees and believes as he sees and believes it, the defective earnestness of his presentation will cause an imperfect sympathy in us. He must believe what he says, or we shall not believe it. Insincerity is always weakness; sincerity even in error is strength. This is not so obvious a principle as the first; at any rate it is one more profoundly disregarded by writers.

Finally, unless the writer has grace—the principle of Beauty I have named it—enabling him to give some aesthetic charm to his presentation, were it only the charm of well-arranged material, and well-constructed sentences, a charm sensible through all the intricacies of COMPOSITION and of STYLE, he will not do justice to his powers, and will either fail to make his work acceptable, or will very seriously limit its success. The amount of influence issuing from this principle of Beauty will, of course, be greatly determined by the more or less aesthetic nature of the work.

Books minister to our knowledge, to our guidance, and to our delight, by their truth, their uprightness, and their art. Truth is the aim of Literature. Sincerity is moral truth. Beauty is aesthetic truth. How rigorously these three principles determine the success of all works whatever, and how rigorously every departure from them, no matter how slight, determines proportional failure, with the inexorable sequence of a physical law, it will be my endeavour to prove in the chapters which are to follow.

Chapter 11
The Principle of Vision.

I.

All good Literature rests primarily on insight. All bad Literature rests upon imperfect insight, or upon imitation, which may be defined as seeing at second-hand.

There are men of clear insight who never become authors: some, because no sufficient solicitation from internal or external impulses makes them bond their energies to the task of giving literary expression to their thoughts; and some, because they lack the adequate powers of literary expression. But no man, be his felicity and facility of expression what they may, ever produces good Literature unless he sees for himself, and sees clearly. It is the very claim and purpose of Literature to show others what they failed to see. Unless a man sees this clearly for himself how can he show it to others?

Literature delivers tidings of the world within and the world without. It tells of the facts which have been witnessed, reproduces the emotions which have been felt. It places before the reader symbols which represent the absent facts, or the relations of these to other facts; and by the vivid presentation of the symbols of emotion kindles the emotive sympathy of readers. The art of selecting the fitting symbols, and of so arranging them as to be intelligible and kindling, distinguishes the great writer from the great thinker; it is an art which also relies on clear insight.

The value of the tidings brought by Literature is determined by their authenticity. At all times the air is noisy with rumours, but the real business of life is transacted on clear insight and authentic speech. False tidings and idle rumours may for an hour clamorously usurp attention, because they are believed to be true; but the cheat is soon discovered, and the rumour dies. In like manner Literature which is unauthentic may succeed as long as it is believed to be true: that is, so long as our intellects have not discovered the falseness of its pretensions, and our feelings have not disowned sympathy with its expressions. These may be truisms, but they are constantly disregarded. Writers have seldom any steadfast conviction that it is of primary necessity for them to deliver tidings about what they themselves have seen and felt. Perhaps their intimate consciousness assures them that what they have seen or felt is neither new nor important. It may not be new, it may not be intrinsically important; nevertheless, if authentic, it has its value, and a far greater value than anything reported by them at second-hand. We cannot demand from every man that he have unusual depth of insight or exceptional experience; but we demand of him that he give us of his best, and his best cannot be another's. The facts seen through the vision of another, reported on the witness of another, may be true, but the reporter cannot vouch for them. Let the original observer speak for himself. Otherwise only rumours are set afloat. If you have never seen an acid combine with a base you cannot instructively speak to me of salts; and this, of course, is true in a more emphatic degree with reference to more complex matters.

Personal experience is the basis of all real Literature. The writer must have thought the thoughts, seen the objects (with bodily or mental vision), and felt the feelings; otherwise he can have no power over us. Importance does not depend on rarity so much as on authenticity. The massacre of a distant tribe, which is heard through the report of others, falls far below the heart-shaking effect of a murder committed in our presence. Our sympathy with the unknown victim may originally have been as torpid as that with the unknown tribe; but it has been kindled by the swift and vivid suggestions of details visible to us as spectators; whereas a severe and continuous effort of imagination is needed to call up the kindling suggestions of the distant massacre.

So little do writers appreciate the importance of direct vision and experience, that they are in general silent about what they themselves have seen and felt, copious in reporting the experience of others. Nay, they are urgently prompted to say what they know others think, and what consequently they themselves may be expected to think. They are as if dismayed at their own individuality, and suppress all traces of it in order to catch the general tone. Such men may, indeed, be of service in the ordinary commerce of Literature as distributors. All I wish to point out is that they are distributors, not producers. The commerce may be served by second-hand reporters, no less than by original seers; but we must understand this service to be commercial and not literary. The common stock of knowledge gains from it no addition. The man who detects a new fact, a new property in a familiar substance, adds to the science of the age; but the man who expounds the whole system of the universe on the reports of others, unenlightened by new conceptions of his own, does not add a grain to the common store. Great writers may all be known by their solicitude about authenticity. A common incident, a simple phenomenon, which has been a part of their experience, often undergoes what may be called "a transfiguration" in their souls, and issues in the form of Art; while many world-agitating events in which they have not been acters, or majestic phenomena of which they were never spectators, are by them left to the unhesitating incompetence of writers who imagine that fine subjects make fine works. Either the great writer leaves such materials untouched, or he employs them as the vehicle of more cherished, because more authenticated tidings,—he paints the ruin of an empire as the scenic background for his picture of the distress of two simple hearts. The inferior writer, because he lays no emphasis on authenticity, cannot understand this avoidance of imposing themes. Condemned by naive incapacity to be a reporter, and not a seer, he hopes to shine by the reflected glory of his subjects. It is natural in him to mistake ambitious art for high art. He does not feel that the best is the highest.

I do not assert that inferior writers abstain from the familiar and trivial. On the contrary, as imitators, they imitate everything which great writers have shown to be sources of interest. But their bias is towards great subjects. They make no new ventures in the direction of personal experience. They are silent on all that they have really seen for themselves. Unable to see the deep significance of what is common, they spontaneously turn towards the uncommon.

There is, at the present day, a fashion in Literature, and in Art generally, which is very deporable, and which may, on a superficial glance, appear at variance with what has just been said. The fashion is that of coat-and-waistcoat realism, a creeping timidity of invention, moving almost exclusively amid scenes of drawing-room existence, with all the reticences and pettinesses of drawing-room conventions. Artists have become photographers, and have turned the camera upon the vulgarities of life, instead of representing the more impassioned movements of life. The majority of books and pictures are addressed to our lower faculties; they make no effort as they have no power to stir our deeper emotions by the contagion of great ideas. Little that makes life noble and solemn is reflected in the Art of our day; to amuse a languid audience seems its highest aim. Seeing this, some of my readers may ask whether the artists have not been faithful to the law I have expounded, and chosen to paint the small things they have seen, rather than the great things they have not seen? The answer is simple. For the most part the artists have not painted what they have seen, but have been false and conventional in their pretended realism. And whenever they have painted truly, they have painted successfully. The authenticity of their work has given it all the value which in the nature of things such work could have. Titian's portrait of "The Young Man with a Glove" is a great work of art, though not of great art. It is infinitely higher than a portrait of Cromwell, by a painter unable to see into the great soul of Cromwell, and to make us see it; but it is infinitely lower than Titian's "Tribute Money," "Peter the Martyr," or the "Assumption." Tennyson's "Northern Farmer" is incomparably greater as a poem than Mr. Bailey's ambitious "Festus;" but the "Northern Farmer" is far below "Ulysses" or "Guinevere," because moving on a lower level, and recording the facts of a lower life.

Insight is the first condition of Art. Yet many a man who has never been beyond his village will be silent about that which he knows well, and will fancy himself called upon to speak of the tropics or the Andes—-on the reports of others. Never having seen a greater man than the parson and the squire and not having seen into them—he selects Cromwell and Plato, Raphael and Napoleon, as his models, in the vain belief that these impressive personalities will make his work impressive. Of course I am speaking figuratively. By "never having been beyond his village," I understand a mental no less than topographical limitation. The penetrating sympathy of genius will, even from a village, traverse the whole world. What I mean is, that unless by personal experience, no matter through what avenues, a man has gained clear insight into the facts of life, he cannot successfully place them before us; and whatever insight he has gained, be it of important or of unimportant facts, will be of value if truly reproduced. No sunset is precisely similar to another, no two souls are affected by it in a precisely similar way. Thus may the commonest phenomenon have a novelty. To the eye that can read aright there is an infinite variety even in the most ordinary human being. But to the careless indiscriminating eye all individuality is merged in a misty generality. Nature and men yield nothing new to such a mind. Of what avail is it for a man to walk out into the tremulous mists of morning, to watch the slow sunset, and wait for the rising stars, if he can tell us nothing about these but what others have already told us—-if he feels nothing but what others have already felt? Let a man look for himself and tell truly what he sees. We will listen to that. We must listen to it, for its very authenticity has a subtle power of compulsion. What others have seen and felt we can learn better from their own lips.

II.

I have not yet explained in any formal manner what the nature of that insight is which constitutes what I have named the Principle of Vision; although doubtless the reader has gathered its meaning from the remarks already made. For the sake of future applications of the principle to the various questions of philosophical criticism which must arise in the course of this inquiry, it may be needful here to explain (as I have already explained elsewhere) how the chief intellectual operations—

Perception, Inference, Reasoning, and Imagination—may be viewed as so many forms of mental vision.

Perception, as distinguished from Sensation, is the presentation before Consciousness of the details which once were present in conjunction with the object at this moment affecting Sense. These details are inferred to be still in conjunction with the object, although not revealed to Sense. Thus when an apple is perceived by me, who merely see it, all that Sense reports is of a certain coloured surface: the roundness, the firmness, the fragrance, and the taste of the apple are not present to Sense, but are made present to Consciousness by the act of Perception. The eye sees a certain coloured surface; the mind sees at the same instant many other co-existent but unapparent facts—it reinstates in their due order these unapparent facts. Were it not for this mental vision supplying the deficiencies of ocular vision, the coloured surface would be an enigma. But the suggestion of Sense rapidly recalls the experiences previously associated with the object. The apparent facts disclose the facts that are unapparent.

Inference is only a higher form of the same process. We look from the window, see the dripping leaves and the wet ground, and infer that rain has fallen. It is on inferences of this kind that all knowledge depends. The extension of the known to the unknown, of the apparent to the unapparent, gives us Science. Except in the grandeur of its sweep, the mind pursues the same course in the interpretation of geological facts as in the interpretation of the ordinary incidents of daily experience. To read the pages of the great Stone Book, and to perceive from the wet streets that rain has recently fallen, are forms of the same intellectual process. In the one case the inference traverses immeasurable spaces of time, connecting the apparent facts with causes (unapparent facts) similar to those which have been associated in experience with such results; in the other case the inference connects wet streets and swollen gutters with causes which have been associated in experience with such results. Let the inference span with its mighty arch a myriad of years, or link together the events of a few minutes, in each case the arch rises from the ground of familiar facts, and reaches an antecedent which is known to be a cause capable of producing them.

The mental vision by which in Perception we see the unapparent details—-i.e, by which sensations formerly co-existing with the one now affecting us are reinstated under the form of ideas which REPRESENT the objects—is a process implied in all Ratiocination, which also presents an IDEAL SERIES, such as would be a series of sensations, if the objects themselves were before us. A chain of reasoning is a chain of inferences: IDEAL presentations of objects and relations not apparent to Sense, or not presentable to Sense. Could we realise all the links in this chain, by placing the objects in their actual order as a VISIBLE series, the reasoning would be a succession of perceptions. Thus the path of a planet is seen by reason to be an ellipse. It would be perceived as a fact, if we were in a proper position and endowed with the requisite means of following the planet in its course; but not having this power, we are reduced to infer the unapparent points in its course from the points which are apparent. We see them mentally. Correct reasoning is the ideal assemblage of objects in their actual order of co-existence and succession. It is seeing with the mind's eye. False reasoning is owing to some misplacement of the order of objects, or to the omission of some links in the chain, or to the introduction of objects not properly belonging to the series. It is distorted or defective vision. The terrified traveller sees a highwayman in what is really a sign-post in the twilight; and in the twilight of knowledge, the terrified philosopher sees a Pestilence foreshadowed by an eclipse.

Let attention also be called to one great source of error, which is also a great source of power, namely, that much of our thinking is carried on by signs instead of images. We use words as signs of objects; these suffice to carry on the train of inference, when very few images of the objects are called up. Let any one attend to his thoughts and he will be surprised to find how rare and indistinct in general are the images of objects which arise before his mind. If he says "I shall take a cab and get to the railway by the shortest cut," it is ten to one that he forms no image of cab or railway, and but a very vague image of the streets through which the shortest cut will lead. Imaginative minds see images where ordinary minds see nothing but signs: this is a source of power; but it is also a source of weakness; for in the practical affairs of life, and in the theoretical investigations of philosophy, a too active imagination is apt to distract the attention and scatter the energies of the mind.

In complex trains of thought signs are indispensable. The images, when called up, are only vanishing suggestions: they disappear before they are more than half formed. And yet it is because signs are thus substituted for images (paper transacting the business of money) that we are so easily imposed upon by verbal fallacies and meaningless phrases. A scientific man of some eminence was once taken in by a wag, who gravely asked him whether he had read Bunsen's paper on the MALLEABILITY of light. He confessed that he had not read it: "Bunsen sent it to me, but I've not had time to look into it."

The degree in which each mind habitually substitutes signs for images will be, CETERIS PARIBUS, the degree in which it is liable to error. This is not contradicted by the fact that mathematical, astronomical, and physical reasonings may, when complex, be carried on more suecessfully by the employment of signs; because in these cases the signs themselves accurately represent the abstractness of the relations. Such sciences deal only with relations, and not with objects; hence greater simplification ensures greater accuracy. But no sooner do we quit this sphere of abstractions to enter that of concrete things, than the use of symbols becomes a source of weakness. Vigorous and effective minds habitually deal with concrete images. This is notably the case with poets and great literates. Their vision is keener than that of other men. However rapid and remote their flight of thought, it is a succession of images, not of abstractions. The details which give significance, and which by us are seen vaguely as through a vanishing mist, are by them seen in sharp outlines. The image which to us is a mere suggestion, is to them almost as vivid as the object. And it is because they see vividly that they can paint effectively.

Most readers will recognise this to be true of poets, but will doubt its application to philosophers, because imperfect psychology and unscientific criticism have disguised the identity of intellectual processes until it has become a paradox to say that imagination is not less indispensable to the philosopher than to the poet. The paradox falls directly we restate the proposition thus: both poet and philosopher draw their power from the energy of their mental vision—an energy which disengages the mind from the somnolence of habit and from the pressure of obtrusive sensations. In general men are passive under Sense and the routine of habitual inferences. They are unable to free themselves from the importunities of the apparent facts and apparent relations which solicit their attention; and when they make room for unapparent facts it is only for those which are familiar to their minds. Hence they can see little more than what they have been taught to see; they can only think what they have been taught to think. For independent vision, and original conception, we must go to children and men of genius. The spontaneity of the one is the power of the other. Ordinary men live among marvels and feel no wonder, grow familiar with objects and learn nothing new about them. Then comes an independent mind which sees; and it surprises us to find how servile we have been to habit and opinion, how blind to what we also might have seen, had we used our eyes. The link, so long hidden, has now been made visible to us. We hasten to make it visible to others. But the flash of light which revealed that obscured object does not help us to discover others. Darkness still conceals much that we do not even suspect. We continue our routine. We always think our views correct and complete; if we thought otherwise they would cease to be our views; and when the man of keener insight discloses our error, and reveals relations hitherto unsuspected, we learn to see with his eyes and exclaim: "Now surely we have got the truth."

III.

A child is playing with a piece of paper and brings it near the flame of a candle; another child looks on. Both are completely absorbed by the objects, both are ignorant or oblivious of the relation between the combustible object and the flame: a relation which becomes apparent only when the paper is alight. What is called the thoughtlessness of childhood prevents their seeing this unapparent fact; it is a fact which has not been sufficiently impressed upon their experience so as to form an indissoluble element in their conception of the two in juxtaposition. Whereas in the mind of the nurse this relation is so vividly impressed that no sooner does the paper approach the flame than the unapparent fact becomes almost as visible as the objects, and a warning is given. She sees what the children do not, or cannot see. It has become part of her organised experience.

The superiority of one mind over another depends on the rapidity with which experiences are thus organised. The superiority may be general or special: it may manifest itself in a power of assimilating very various experiences, so as to have manifold relations familiar to it, or in a power of assimilating very special relations, so as to constitute a distinctive aptitude for one branch of art or science. The experience which is thus organised must of course have been originally a direct object of consciousness, either as an impressive fact or impressive inference. Unless the paper had been seen to burn, no one could know that contact with flame would consume it. By a vivid remembrance the experience of the past is made available to the present, so that we do not need actually to burn paper once more,—we see the relation mentally. In like manner Newton did not need to go through the demonstrations of many complex problems, they flashed upon him as he read the propositions; they were seen by him in that rapid glance, as they would have been made visible through the slower process of demonstration. A good chemist does not need to test many a proposition by bringing actual gases or acids into operation, and seeing the result; he FORESEES the result: his mental vision of the objects and their properties is so keen, his experience is so organised, that the result which would be visible in an experiment, is visible to him in an intuition. A fine poet has no need of the actual presence of men and women under the fluctuating impatience of emotion, or under the steadfast hopelessness of grief; he needs no setting sun before his window, under it no sullen sea. These are all visible, and their fluctuations are visible. He sees the quivering lip, the agitated soul; he hears the aching cry, and the dreary wash of waves upon the beach.

The writer who pretends to instruct us should first assure himself that he has clearer vision of the things he speaks of,—knows them and their qualities, if not better than we, at least with some distinctive knowledge. Otherwise he should announce himself as a mere echo, a middleman, a distributor.

Our need is for more light. This can be given only by an independent seer who

"Lends a precious seeing to the eye."

All great authors are seers. "Perhaps if we should meet Shakspeare," says Emerson, "we should not be conscious of any steep inferiority: no, but of great equality; only he possessed a strange skill of using, of classifying his facts, which we lacked. For, notwithstanding our utter incapacity to preduce anything like HAMLET or OTHELLO, we see the perfect reception this wit and immense knowledge of life and liquid eloquence find in us all." This aggrandisement of our common stature rests on questionable ground. If our capacity of being moved by Shakspeare discloses a community, our incapacity of producing HAMLET no less discloses our inferiority. It is certain that could we meet Shakspeare we should find him strikingly like ourselves—-with the same faculties, the same sensibilities, though not in the same degree. The secret of his power over us lies, of course, in our having the capacity to appreciate him. Yet we seeing him in the unimpassioned moods of daily life, it is more than probable that we should see nothing in him but what was ordinary; nay, in some qualities he would seem inferior. Heroes require a perspective. They are men who look superhuman only when elevated on the pedestals of their achievements. In ordinary life they look like ordinary men; not that they are of the common mould, but seem so because their uncommon qualities are not then called forth. Superiority requires an occasion. The common man is helpless in an emergency: assailed by contradictory suggestions, or confused by his incapacity, he cannot see his way. The hour of emergency finds a hero calm and strong, and strong because calm and clear-sighted; he sees what can be done, and does it. This is often a thing of great simplicity, so that we marvel others did not see it. Now it has been done, and proved successful, many underrate its value, thinking that they also would have done precisely the same thing. The world is more just. It refuses to men unassailed by the difficulties of a situation the glory they have not earned. The world knows how easy most things appear when they have once been done. We can all make the egg stand on end after Columbus.

Shakspeare, then, would probably not impress us with a sense of our inferiority if we were to meet him tomorrow. Most likely we should be bitterly disappointed; because, having formed our conception of him as the man who wrote HAMLET and OTHELLO we forget that these were not the preducts of his ordinary moods, but the manifestations of his power at white heat. In ordinary moods he must be very much as ordinary men, and it is in these we meet him. How notorious is the astonishment of friends and associates when any man's achievements suddenly emerge into renown. "They could never have believed it." Why should they? Knowing him only as one of their circle, and not being gifted with the penetration which discerns a latent energy, but only with the vision which discerns apparent results, they are taken by surprise. Nay, so biased are we by superficial judgments, that we frequently ignore the palpable fact of achieved excellence simply because we cannot reconcile it with our judgment of the man who achieved it. The deed has been done, the work written, the picture painted; it is before the world, and the world is ringing with applause. There is no doubt whatever that the man whose name is in every mouth did the work; but because our personal impressions of him do not correspond with our conceptions of a powerful man, we abate or withdraw our admiration, and attribute his success to lucky accident. This blear-eyed, taciturn, timid man, whose knowledge of many things is manifestly imperfect, whose inaptitude for many things is apparent, can HE be the creator of such glorious works? Can HE be the large and patient thinker, the delicate humourist, the impassioned poet? Nature seems to have answered this question for us; yet so little are we inclined to accept Nature's emphatic testimony on this point, that few of us ever see without disappointment the man whose works have revealed his greatness.

It stands to reason that we should not rightly appreciate Shakspeare if we were to meet him simply because we should meet him as an ordinary man, and not as the author of HAMLET. Yet if we had a keen insight we should detect even in his quiet talk the marks of an original mind. We could not, of course, divine, without evidence, how deep and clear his insight, how mighty his power over grand representative symbols, how prodigal his genius: these only could appear on adequate occasions. But we should notice that he had an independent way of looking at things. He would constantly bring before us some latent fact, some unsuspected relation, some resemblance between dissimilar things. We should feel that his utterances were not echoes. If therefore, in these moments of equable serenity, his mind glancing over trivial things saw them with great clearness, we might infer that in moments of intense activity his mind gazing steadfastly on important things, would see wonderful visions, where to us all was vague and shifting. During our quiet walk with him across the fields he said little, or little that was memorable; but his eye was taking in the varying forms and relations of objects, and slowly feeding his mind with images. The common hedge-row, the gurgling brook, the waving corn, the shifting cloud-architecture, and the sloping uplands, have been seen by us a thousand times, but they show us nothing new; they have been seen by him a thousand times, and each time with fresh interest, and fresh discovery. If he describe that walk he will surprise us with revelations: we can then and thereafter see all that he points out; but we needed his vision to direct our own. And it is one of the incalculable influences of poetry that each new revelation is an education of the eye and the feelings. We learn to see and feel Nature in a far clearer and profounder way, now that we have been taught to look by poets. The incurious unimpassioned gaze of the Alpine peasant on the scenes which mysteriously and profoundly affect the cultivated tourist, is the gaze of one who has never been taught to look. The greater sensibility of educated Europeans to influences which left even the poetic Greeks unmoved, is due to the directing vision of successive poets.

The great difficulty which besets us all—Shakspeares and others, but Shakspeares less than others—-is the difficulty of disengaging the mind from the thraldom of sensation and habit, and escaping from the pressure of objects immediately present, or of ideas which naturally emerge, linked together as they are by old associations. We have to see anew, to think anew. It requires great vigour to escape from the old and spontaneously recurrent trains of thought. And as this vigour is native, not acquired, my readers may, perhaps, urge the futility of expounding with so much pains a principle of success in Literature which, however indispensable, must be useless as a guide; they may object that although good Literature rests on insight, there is nothing to be gained by saying "unless a man have the requisite insight he will not succeed." But there is something to be gained. In the first place, this is an analytical inquiry into the conditions of success: it aims at discriminating the leading principles which inevitably determine success. In the second place, supposing our analysis of the conditions to be correct, practical guidance must follow. We cannot, it is true, gain clearness of vision simply by recognising its necessity; but by recognising its necessity we are taught to seek for it as a primary condition of success; we are forced to come to an understanding with ourselves as to whether we have or have not a distinct vision of the thing we speak of, whether we are seers or reporters, whether the ideas and feelings have been thought and felt by us as part and parcel of our own individual experience, or have been echoed by us from the books and conversation of others? We can always ask, are we painting farm-houses or fairies because these are genuine visions of our own, or only because farm-houses and fairies have been successfully painted by others, and are poetic material?

The man who first saw an acid redden a vegetable-blue, had something to communicate; and the man who first saw (mentally) that all acids redden vegetable-blues, had something to communicate. But no man can do this again. In the course of his teaching he may have frequently to report the fact; but this repetition is not of much value unless it can be made to disclose some new relation. And so of other and more complex cases. Every sincere man can determine for himself whether he has any authentic tidings to communicate; and although no man can hope to discover much that is actually new, he ought to assure himself that even what is old in his work has been authenticated by his own experience. He should not even speak of acids reddening vegetable-blues upon mere hearsay, unless he is speaking figuratively. All his facts should have been verified by himself, all his ideas should have been thought by himself. In proportion to the fulfilment of this condition will be his success; in proportion to its non-fulfilment, his failure.

Literature in its vast extent includes writers of three different classes, and in speaking of success we must always be understood to mean the acceptance each writer gains in his own class; otherwise a flashy novelist might seem more successful than a profound poet; a clever compiler more successful than an original discoverer.

The Primary Class is composed of the born seers—men who see for themselves and who originate. These are poets, philosophers, discoverers. The Secondary Class is composed of men less puissant in faculty, but genuine also in their way, who travel along the paths opened by the great originaters, and also point out many a side-path and shorter cut. They reproduce and vary the materials furnished by others, but they do this, not as echoes only, they authenticate their tidings, they take care to see what the discoverers have taught them to see, and in consequence of this clear vision they are enabled to arrange and modify the materials so as to produce new results. The Primary Class is composed of men of genius; the Secondary Class of men of talent. It not unfrequently happens, especially in philosophy and science, that the man of talent may confer a lustre on the original invention; he takes it up a nugget and lays it down a coin. Finally, there is the largest class of all, comprising the Imitators in Art, and the Compilers in Philosophy. These bring nothing to the general stock. They are sometimes (not often) useful; but it is as cornfactors, not as corn-growers. They sometimes do good service by distributing knowledge where otherwise it might never penetrate; but in general their work is more hurtful than beneficial: hurtful, because it is essentially bad work, being insincere work, and because it stands in the way of better work.

Even among Imitaters and Compilers there are almost infinite degrees of merit and demerit: echoes of echoes reverberating echoes in endless succession; compilations of all degrees of worth and worthlessness. But, as will be shown hereafter, even in this lower sphere the worth of the work is strictly proportional to the Vision, Sincerity, and Beauty; so that an imitator whose eye is keen for the forms he imitates, whose speech is honest, and whose talent has grace, will by these very virtues rise almost to the Secondary Class, and will secure an honourable success.

I have as yet said but little, and that incidentally, of the part played by the Principle of Vision in Art. Many readers who will admit the principle in Science and Philosophy, may hesitate in extending it to Art, which, as they conceive, draws its inspirations from the Imagination. Properly understood there is no discrepancy between the two opinions; and in the next chapter I shall endeavour to show how Imagination is only another form of this very Principle of Vision which we have been considering.

❋❋❋

Chapter 111
Of Vision in Art.

I.

There are many who will admit, without hesitation, that in Philosophy what I have called the Principle of Vision holds an important rank, because the mind must necessarily err in its speculations unless it clearly sees facts and relations; but there are some who will hesitate before admitting the principle to a similar rank in Art, because, as they conceive, Art is independent of the truth of facts, and is swayed by the autocratic power of Imagination.

It is on this power that our attention should first be arrested; the more so because it is usually spoken of in vague rhapsodical language, with intimations of its being something peculiarly mysterious. There are few words more abused. The artist is called a creator, which in one sense he is; and his creations are said to be produced by processes wholly unallied to the creations of Philosophy, which they are not. Hence it is a paradox to speak of the "Principia," as a creation demanding severe and continuous exercise of the imagination; but it is only a paradox to those who have never analysed the processes of artistic and philosophic creation.

I am far from desiring to innovate in language, or to raise interminable discussions respecting the terms in general use. Nevertheless we have here to deal with questions that lie deeper than mere names. We have to examine processes, and trace, if possible, the methods of intellectual activity pursued in all branches of Literature; and we must not suffer our course to be obstructed by any confusion in terms that can be cleared up. We may respect the demarcations established by usage, but we must ascertain, if possible, the fundamental affinities. There is, for instance, a broad distinction between Science and Art, which, so far from requiring to be effaced, requires to be emphasised: it is that in Science the paramount appeal is to the Intellect--its purpose being instruction; in Art, the paramount appeal is to the Emotions—its purpose being pleasure. A work of Art must of course indirectly appeal to the Intellect, and a work of Science will also indirectly appeal to the Feelings; nevertheless a poem on the stars and a treatise on astronomy have distinct aims and distinct methods. But having recognised the broadly-marked differences, we are called upon to ascertain the underlying resemblances. Logic and Imagination belong equally to both. It is only because men have been attracted by the differences that they have overlooked the not less important affinities. Imagination is an intellectual process common to Philosophy and Art; but in each it is allied with different processes, and directed to different ends; and hence, although the "Principia" demanded an imagination of not less vivid and sustained power than was demanded by "Othello," it would be very false psychology to infer that the mind of Newton was competent to the creation of "Othello," or the mind of Shakspeare capable of producing the "Principia." They were specifically different minds; their works were specifically different. But in both the imagination was intensely active. Newton had a mind predominantly ratiocinative: its movement was spontaneously towards the abstract relations of things. Shakspeare had a mind predominantly emotive, the intellect always moving in alliance with the feelings, and spontaneously fastening upon the concrete facts in preference to their abstract relations. Their mental Vision was turned towards images of different orders, and it moved in alliance with different faculties; but this Vision was the cardinal quality of both. Dr. Johnson was guilty of a surprising fallacy in saying that a great mathematician might also be a great poet: "Sir, a man can walk east as far as he can walk west." True, but mathematics and poetry do not differ as east and west; and he would hardly assert that a man who could walk twenty miles could therefore swim that distance.

The real state of the case is somewhat obscured by our observing that many men of science, and some even eminent as teachers and reporters, display but slender claims to any unusual vigour of imagination. It must be owned that they are often slightly dull; and in matters of Art are not unfrequently blockheads. Nay, they would themselves repel it as a slight if the epithet "imaginative" were applied to them; it would seem to impugn their gravity, to cast doubts upon their accuracy. But such men are the cisterns, not the fountains, of Science. They rely upon the knowledge already organised; they do not bring accessions to the common stock. They are not investigators, but imitators; they are not discoverers—inventors. No man ever made a discovery (he may have stumbled on one) without the exercise of as much imagination as, employed in another direction and in alliance with other faculties, would have gone to the creation of a poem. Every one who has seriously investigated a novel question, who has really interrogated Nature with a view to a distinct answer, will bear me out in saying that it requires intense and sustained effort of imagination. The relations of sequence among the phenomena must be seen; they are hidden; they can only be seen mentally; a thousand suggestions rise before the mind, but they are recognised as old suggestions, or as inadequate to reveal what is sought; the experiments by which the problem may be solved have to be imagined; and to imagine a good experiment is as difficult as to invent a good fable, for we must have distinctly PRESENT—clear mental vision—the known qualities and relations of all the objects, and must see what will be the effect of introducing some new qualifying agent. If any one thinks this is easy, let him try it: the trial will teach him a lesson respecting the methods of intellectual activity not without its use. Easy enough, indeed, is the ordinary practice of experiment, which is either a mere repetition or variation of experiments already devised (as ordinary story-tellers re-tell the stories of others), or else a haphazard, blundering way of bringing phenomena together, to see what will happen. To invent is another process. The discoverer and the poet are inventors; and they are so because their mental vision detects the unapparent, unsuspected facts, almost as vividly as ocular vision rests on the apparent and familiar.

It is the special aim of Philosophy to discover and systematise the abstract relations of things; and for this purpose it is forced to allow the things themselves to drop out of sight, fixing attention solely on the quality immediately investigated, to the neglect of all other qualities. Thus the philosopher, having to appreciate the mass, density, refracting power, or chemical constitution of some object, finds he can best appreciate this by isolating it from every other detail. He abstracts this one quality from the complex bundle of qualities which constitute the object, and he makes this one stand for the whole. This is a necessary simplification. If all the qualities were equally present to his mind, his vision would be perplexed by their multiple suggestions. He may follow out the relations of each in turn, but he cannot follow them out together.

The aim of the poet is very different. He wishes to kindle the emotions by the suggestion of objects themselves; and for this purpose he must present images of the objects rather than of any single quality. It is true that he also must exercise a power of abstraction and selection, tie cannot without confusion present all the details. And it is here that the fine selective instinct of the true artist shows itself, in knowing what details to present and what to omit. Observe this: the abstraction of the philosopher is meant to keep the object itself, with its perturbing suggestions, out of sight, allowing only one quality to fill the field of vision; whereas the abstraction of the poet is meant to bring the object itself into more vivid relief, to make it visible by means of the selected qualities. In other words, the one aims at abstract symbols, the other at picturesque effects. The one can carry on his deductions by the aid of colourless signs, X or Y. The other appeals to the emotions through the symbols which will most vividly express the real objects in their relations to our sensibilities.

Imagination is obviously active in both. From known facts the philosopher infers the facts that are unapparent. He does so by an effort of imagination (hypothesis) which has to be subjected to verification: he makes a mental picture of the unapparent fact, and then sets about to prove that his picture does in some way correspond with the reality. The correctness of his hypothesis and verification must depend on the clearness of his vision. Were all the qualities of things apparent to Sense, there would be no longer any mystery. A glance would be Science. But only some of the facts are visible; and it is because we see little, that we have to imagine much. We see a feather rising in the air, and a quill, from the same bird, sinking to the ground: these contradictory reports of sense lead the mind astray; or perhaps excite a desire to know the reason. We cannot see,—we must imagine,—the unapparent facts. Many mental pictures may be formed, but to form the one which corresponds with the reality requires great sagacity and a very clear vision of known facts. In trying to form this mental picture we remember that when the air is removed the feather fails as rapidly as the quill, and thus we see that the air is the cause of the feather's rising; we mentally see the air pushing under the feather, and see it almost as plainly as if the air were a visible mass thrusting the feather upwards.

From a mistaken appreciation of the real process this would by few be called an effort of Imagination. On the contrary some "wild hypothesis" would be lauded as imaginative in proportion as it departed from all suggestion of experience, i.e. real mental vision. To have imagined that the feather rose owing to its "specific lightness," and that the quill fell owing to its "heaviness," would to many appear a more decided effort of the imaginative faculty. Whereas it is no effort of that faculty at all; it is simply naming differently the facts it pretends to explain. To imagine—-to form an image—we must have the numerous relations of things present to the mind, and see the objects in their actual order. In this we are of course greatly aided by the mass of organised experience, which allows us rapidly to estimate the relations of gravity or affinity just as we remember that fire burns and that heated bodies expand. But be the aid great or small, and the result victorious or disastrous, the imaginative process is always the same.

There is a slighter strain on the imagination of the poet, because of his greater freedom. He is not, like the philosopher, limited to the things which are, or were. His vision includes things which might be, and things which never were. The philosopher is not entitled to assume that Nature sympathises with man; he must prove the fact to be so if he intend making any use of it ;—we admit no deductions from unproved assumptions. But the poet is at perfect liberty to assume this; and having done so, he paints what would be the manifestations of this sympathy. The naturalist who should describe a hippogriff would incur the laughing scorn of Europe; but the poet feigns its existence, and all Europe is delighted when it rises with Astolfo in the air. We never pause to ask the poet whether such an animal exists. He has seen it, and we see it with his eyes. Talking trees do not startle us in Virgil and Tennyson. Puck and Titania, Hamlet and Falstaff, are as true for us as Luther and Napoleon so long as we are in the realm of Art. We grant the poet a free privilege because he will use it only for our pleasure. In Science pleasure is not an object, and we give no licence.

Philosophy and Art both render the invisible visible by imagination. Where Sense observes two isolated objects, Imagination discloses two related objects. This relation is the nexus visible. We had not seen it before; it is apparent now. Where we should only see a calamity the poet makes us see a tragedy. Where we could only see a sunrise he enables us to see

"Day like a mighty river flowing in."

Imagination is not the exclusive appanage of artists, but belongs in varying degrees to all men. It is simply the power of forming images. Supplying the energy of Sense where Sense cannot reach, it brings into distinctness the facts, obscure or occult, which are grouped round an object or an idea, but which are not actually present to Sense. Thus, at the aspect of a windmill, the mind forms images of many characteristic facts relating to it; and the kind of images will depend very much on the general disposition, or particular mood, of the mind affected by the object: the painter, the poet, and the moralist will have different images suggested by the presence of the windmill or its symbol. There are indeed sluggish minds so incapable of self-evolved activity, and so dependent on the immediate suggestions of Sense, as to be almost destitute of the power of forming distinct images beyond the immediate circle of sensuous associations; and these are rightly named unimaginative minds; but in all minds of energetic activity, groups and clusters of images, many of them representing remote relations, spontaneously present themselves in conjunction with objects or their symbols. It should, however, be borne in mind that Imagination can only recall what Sense has previously impressed. No man imagines any detail of which he has not previously had direct or indirect experience. Objects as fictitious as mermaids and hippogriffs are made up from the gatherings of Sense.

"Made up from the gatherings of Sense" is a phrase which may seem to imply some peculiar plastic power such as is claimed exclusively for artists: a power not of simple recollection, but of recollection and recombination. Yet this power belongs also to philosophers. To combine the half of a woman with the half of a fish,—to imagine the union as an existing organism,—is not really a different process from that of combining the experience of a chemical action with an electric action, and seeing that the two are one existing fact. When the poet hears the storm-cloud muttering, and sees the moonlight sleeping on the bank, he transfers his experience of human phenomena to the cloud and the moonlight: he personifies, draws Nature within the circle of emotion, and is called a poet. When the philosopher sees electricity in the storm-cloud, and sees the sunlight stimulating vegetable growth, he transfers his experience of physical phenomena to these objects, and draws within the circle of Law phenomena which hitherto have been unclassified. Obviously the imagination has been as active in the one case as in the other; the DIFFERENTIA lying in the purposes of the two, and in the general constltution of the two minds.

It has been noted that there is less strain on the imagination of the poet; but even his greater freedom is not altogether disengaged from the necessity of verification; his images must have at least subjective truth; if they do not accurately correspond with objective realities, they must correspond with our sense of congruity. No poet is allowed the licence of creating images inconsistent with our conceptions. If he said the moonlight burnt the bank, we should reject the image as untrue, inconsistent with our conceptions of moonlight; whereas the gentle repose of the moonlight on the bank readily associates itself with images of sleep.

The often mooted question, What is Imagination? thus receives a very clear and definite answer. It is the power of forming images; it reinstates, in a visible group, those objects which are invisible, either from absence or from imperfection of our senses. That is its generic character. Its specific character, which marks it off from Memory, and which is derived from the powers of selection and recombination, will be expounded further on. Here I only touch upon its chief characteristic, in order to disengage the term from that mysteriousness which writers have usually assigned to it, thereby rendering philosophic criticism impossible. Thus disengaged it may be used with more certainty in an attempt to estimate the imaginative power of various works.

Hitherto the amount of that power has been too frequently estimated according to the extent of DEPARTURE from ordinary experience in the images selected. Nineteen out of twenty would unhesitatingly declare that a hippogriff was a greater effort of imagination than a well-conceived human character; a Peri than a woman; Puck or Titania than Falstaff or Imogen. A description of Paradise extremely unlike any known garden must, it is thought, necessarily be more imaginative than the description of a quiet rural nook. It may be more imaginative; it may be less so.

All depends upon the mind of the poet. To suppose that it must, because of its departure from ordinary experience, is a serious error. The muscular effort required to draw a cheque for a thousand pounds might as reasonably be thought greater than that required for a cheque of five pounds; and much as the one cheque seems to surpass the other in value, the result of presenting both to the bankers may show that the more modest cheque is worth its full five pounds, whereas the other is only so much waste paper. The description of Paradise may be a glittering farrago; the description of the landscape may be full of sweet rural images: the one having a glare of gaslight and Vauxhall splendour; the other having the scent of new-mown hay.

A work is imaginative in virtue of the power of its images over our emotions; not in virtue of any rarity or surprisingness in the images themselves. A Madonna and Child by Fra Angelico is more powerful over our emotions than a Crucifixion by a vulgar artist; a beggar-boy by Murillo is more imaginative than an Assumption by the same painter; but the Assumption by Titian displays far greater imagination than elther. We must guard against the natural tendency to attribute to the artist what is entirely due to accidental conditions. A tropical scene, luxuriant with tangled overgrowth and impressive in the grandeur of its phenomena, may more decisively arrest our attention than an English landscape with its green corn lands and plenteous homesteads. But this superiority of interest is no proof of the artist's superior imagination; and by a spectator familiar with the tropics, greater interest may be felt in the English landscape, because its images may more forcibly arrest his attentlon by their novelty. And were this not so, were the inalienable impressiveness of tropical scenery always to give the poet who described it a superiority in effect, this would not prove the superiority of his imagination. For either he has been familiar with such scenes, and imagines them just as the other poet imagines his English landscape--by an effort of mental vision, calling up the absent objects; or he has merely read the descriptions of others, and from these makes up his picture. It is the same with his rival, who also recalls and recombines. Foolish critics often betray their ignorance by saying that a painter or a writer "only copies what he has seen, or puts down what he has known." They forget that no man imagines what he has not seen or known, and that it is in the SELECTION OF THE CHARACTERISTIC DETAILS that the artistic power is manifested. Those who suppose that familiarity with scenes or characters enables a painter or a novelist to "copy" them with artistic effect, forget the well-known fact that the vast majority of men are painfully incompetent to avail themselves of this familiarity, and cannot form vivid pictures even to themselves of scenes in which they pass their daily lives; and if they could imagine these, they would need the delicate selective instinct to guide them in the admission and omission of details, as well as in the grouping of the images. Let any one try to "copy" the wife or brother he knows so well,—to make a human image which shall speak and act so as to impress strangers with a belief in its truth,—and he will then see that the much-despised reliance on actual experience is not the mechanical procedure it is believed to be. When Scott drew Saladin and Ceaur de Lion he did not really display more imaginative power than when he drew the Mucklebackits, although the majority of readers would suppose that the one demanded a great effort of imagination, whereas the other formed part of his familiar experiences of Scottish life. The mistake here lies in confounding the sources from which the materials were derived with the plastic power of forming these materials into images. More conscious effort may have been devoted to the collection of the materials in the one case than in the other, but that this has nothing to do with the imaginative power employed may readily be proved by an analysis of the intellectual processes of composition. Scott had often been in fishermen's cottages and heard them talk; from the registered experience of a thousand details relating to the life of the poor, their feelings and their thoughts, he gained that material upon which his imagination could work; in the case of Saladin and Ceaur de Lion he had to gain these principally through books and his general experience of life; and the images he formed—the vision he had of Mucklebackit and Saladin—must be set down to his artistic faculty, not to his experience or erudition.

It has been well said by a very imaginative writer, that "when a poet floats in the empyrean, and only takes a bird's-eye view of the earth, some people accept the mere fact of his soaring for sublimity, and mistake his dim vision of earth for proximity to heaven." And in like manner, when a thinker frees himself from all the trammels of fact, and propounds a "bold hypothesis," people mistake the vagabond erratic flights of guessing for a higher range of philosophic power. In truth, the imagination is most tasked when it has to paint pictures which shall withstand the silent criticism of general experience, and to frame hypotheses which shall withstand the confrontation with facts. I cannot here enter into the interesting question of Realism and Idealism in Art, which must be debated in a future chapter; but I wish to call special attention to the psychological fact, that fairies and demons, remote as they are from experience, are not created by a more vigorous effort of imagination than milk maids and poachers. The intensity of vision in the artist and of vividness in his creations are the sole tests of his imaginative power.

II.

If this brief exposition has carried the reader's assent, he will readily apply the principle, and recognise that an artist produces an effect in virtue of the distinctness with which he sees the objects he represents, seeing them not vaguely as in vanishing apparitions, but steadily, and in their most characteristic relations. To this Vision he adds artistic skill with which to make us see. He may have clear conceptions, yet fail to make them clear to us: in this case he has imagination, but is not an artist. Without clear Vision no skill can avail. Imperfect Vision necessitates imperfect representation; words take the place of ideas.

In Young's "Night Thoughts" there are many examples of the PSEUDO-imaginative, betraying an utter want of steady Vision. Here is one:—

"His hand the good man fixes on the skies,
And bids earth roll, nor feels the idle whirl."

"Pause for a moment," remarks a critic, "to realise the image, and the monstrous absurdity of a man's grasping the skies and hanging habitually suspended there, while he contemptuously bids earth roll, warns you that no genuine feeling could have suggested so unnatural a conception." [WESTMINSTER REVIEW, No. cxxxi., p. 27]. It is obvious that if Young had imagined the position he assigned to the good man he would have seen its absurdity; instead of imagining, he allowed the vague transient suggestion of half-nascent images to shape themselves in verse.

Now compare with this a passage in which imagination is really active.

Wordsworth recalls how—

"In November days
When vapours rolling down the valleys made
A lonely scene more lonesome; among the woods
At noon; and mid the calm of summer nights,
When by the margin of the trembling lake

Beneath the gloomy hills homeward I went
In solitude, such intercourse was mine."

There is nothing very grand or impressive in this passage, and therefore it is a better illustration for my purpose. Note how happily the one image, out of a thousand possible images by which November might be characterised, is chosen to call up in us the feeling of the lonely scene; and with what delicate selection the calm of summer nights, the "trembling lake" (an image in an epithet), and the gloomy hills, are brought before us. His boyhood might have furnished him with a hundred different pictures, each as distinct as this; the power is shown in selecting this one—painting it so vividly. He continues:—

"'Twas mine among the fields both day and night
And by the waters, all the summer long.
And in the frosty season, when the sun
Was set, and, visible for many a mile
The cottage windows through the twilight blazed,
I heeded not the summons: happy time
It was indeed for all of us; for me
It was a time of rapture! Clear and loud
The village clock tolled six—I wheeled about,
Proud and exulting like an untired horse
That cares not for his home. All shod with steel
We hissed along the polished ice, in games
Confederate, imitative of the chase
And woodland pleasures—the resounding horn,
The pack loud-chiming and the hunted hare."

There is nothing very felicitous in these lines; yet even here the poet, if languid, is never false. As he proceeds the vision brightens, and the verse becomes instinct with life:—

"So through the darkness and the cold we flew
And not a voice was idle: with the din
Smitten, the precipices rang aloud;
THE LEAFLESS TREES AND EVERY ICY CRAG

TINKLED LIKE IRON; WHILE THE DISTANT HILLS
INTO THE TUMULT SENT AN ALIEN SOUND
OF MELANCHOLY, not unnoticed while the stars
Eastward were sparkling clear, and in the west
The orange sky of evening died away.

"Not seldom from the uproar I retired
Into a silent bay, or sportively
Glanced sideway, leaving the tumultuous throng,
TO CUT ACROSS THE REFLEX OF A STAR;
IMAGE THAT FLYING STILL BEFORE ME gleamed
Upon the glassy plain: and oftentime
When we had given our bodies to the wind
AND ALL THE SHADOWY BANKS ON EITHER SIDE
CAME CREEPING THROUGH THE DARKNESS, spinning still
The rapid line of motion, then at once
Have I reclining back upon my heels
Stopped short; yet still the solitary cliffs
Wheeled by me – even as if the earth had rolled
With visible motion her diurnal round!
Behind me did they stretch in solemn train,
Feebler and feebler, and I stood and watched
Till all was tranquil as a summer sea."

Every poetical reader will feel delight in the accuracy with which the details are painted, and the marvellous clearness with which the whole scene is imagined, both in its objective and subjective relations, i.e., both in the objects seen and the emotions they suggest.

What the majority of modern verse writers call "imagery," is not the product of imagination, but a restless pursuit of comparison, and a lax use of language. Instead of presenting us with an image of the object, they present us with something which they tell us is like the object--which it rarely is. The thing itself has no clear significance to them, it is only a text for the display of their ingenuity. If, however, we turn from poetasters to poets, we see great accuracy in depicting the things themselves or their suggestions, so that we may be certain the things presented themselves in the field of the poet's vision, and were painted because seen. The images arose with sudden vivacity, or were detained long enough to enable their characters to be seized. It is this power of detention to which I would call particular notice, because a valuable practical lesson may be learned through a proper estimate of it. If clear Vision be indispensable to success in Art, all means of securing that clearness should be sought. Now one means is that of detaining an image long enough before the mind to allow of its being seen in all its characteristics. The explanation Newton gave of his discovery of the great law, points in this direction; it was by always thinking of the subject, by keeping it constantly before his mind, that he finally saw the truth. Artists brood over the chaos of their suggestions, and thus shape them into creations. Try and form a picture in your own mind of your early skating experience. It may be that the scene only comes back upon you in shifting outlines, you recall the general facts, and some few particulars are vivid, but the greater part of the details vanish again before they can assume decisive shape; they are but half nascent, or die as soon as born: a wave of recollection washes over the mind, but it quickly retires, leaving no trace behind. This is the common experience. Or it may be that the whole scene flashes upon you with peculiar vividness, so that you see, almost as in actual presence, all the leading characteristics of the picture. Wordsworth may have seen his early days in a succession of vivid flashes, or he may have attained to his distinctness of vision by a steadfast continuity of effort, in which what at first was vague became slowly definite as he gazed. It is certain that only a very imaginative mind could have seen such details as he has gathered together in the lines describing how he

"Cut across the reflex of a star;
Image that flying still before me gleamed
Upon the glassy plain."

The whole description may have been written with great rapidity, or with anxious and tentative labour: the memories of boyish days may have been kindled with a sudden illumination, or they may have grown slowly into the requisite distinctness, detail after detail emerging from the general obscurity, like the appearing stars at night. But whether the poet felt his way to images and epithets, rapidly or slowly, is unimportant; we have to do only with the result; and the result implies, as an absolute condition, that the images were distinct. Only thus could they serve the purposes of poetry, which must arouse in us memories of similar scenes, and kindle emotions of pleasurable experience.

III.

Having cited an example of bad writing consequent on imperfect Vision, and an example of good writing consequent on accurate Vision, I might consider that enough had been done for the immediate purpose of the present chapter; the many other illustrations which the Principle of Vision would require before it could be considered as adequately expounded, I must defer till I come to treat of the application of principles. But before closing this chapter it may be needful to examine some arguments which have a contrary tendency, and imply, or seem to imply, that distinctness of Vision is very far from necessary.

At the outset we must come to an understanding as to this word "image," and endeavour to free the word "vision" from all equivoque. If these words were understood literally there would be an obvious absurdity in speaking of an image of a sound, or of seeing an emotion. Yet if by means of symbols the effect of a sound is produced in us, or the psychological state of any human being is rendered intelligible to us, we are said to have images of these things, which the poet has imagined. It is because the eye is the most valued and intellectual of our senses that the majority of metaphors are borrowed from its sensations. Language, after all, is only the use of symbols, and Art also can only affect us through symbols. If a phrase can summon a terror resembling that summoned by the danger which it indicates, a man is said to see the danger. Sometimes a phrase will awaken more vivid images of danger than would be called up by the actual presence of the dangerous object; because the mind will more readily apprehend the symbols of the phrase than interpret the indications of unassisted sense.

Burke in his "Essay on the Sublime and Beautiful," lays down the proposition that distinctness of imagery is often injurious to the effect of art. "It is one thing," he says, "to make an idea clear, another to make it AFFECTING to the imagination. If I make a drawing of a palace or a temple or a landscape, I present a very clear idea of those objects; but then (allowing for the effect of imitation, which is something) my picture can at most affect only as the palace, temple, or landscape would have affected in reality. On the other hand the most lively and spirited verbal description I can give raises a very obscure and imperfect IDEA of such objects; but then it is in my power to raise a stronger EMOTION by the description than I can do by the best painting. This experience constantly evinces. The proper manner of conveying the AFFECTIONS of the mind from one to the other is by words; there is great insufficiency in all other method of communication; and so far is a clearness of imagery, from being absolutely necessary to an influence upon the passions, that they may be considerably operated upon without presenting any image at all, by certain sounds adapted to that purpose." If by image is meant only what the eye can see, Burke is undoubtedly right. But this is obviously not our restricted meaning of the word when we speak of poetic imagery; and

Burke's error becomes apparent when he proceeds to show that there "are reasons in nature why an obscure idea, when properly conveyed, should be more affecting than the clear." He does not seem to have considered that the idea of an indefinite object can only be properly conveyed by indefinite images; any image of Eternity or Death that pretended to visual distinctness would be false. Having overlooked this, he says, "We do not anywhere meet a more sublime description than this justly celebrated one of Milton, wherein he gives the portrait of Satan with a dignity so suitable to the subject.

"He above the rest
In shape and gesture proudly eminent
Stood like a tower; his form had not yet lost
All her original brightness, nor appeared
Less than archangel ruined and the excess
Of glory obscured: as when the sun new risen
Looks through the horizontal misty air
Shorn of his beams; or from behind the moon
In dim eclipse disastrous twilight sheds
On half the nations; and with fear of change
Perplexes monarchs."

"Here is a very noble picture," adds Burke, "and in what does this poetical picture consist? In images of a tower, an archangel, the sun rising through mists, or an eclipse, the ruin of monarchs, and the revolution of kingdoms." Instead of recognising the imagery here as the source of the power, he says, "The mind is hurried out of itself, [rather a strange result!], by a crowd of great and confused images; which affect because they are crowded and confused For, separate them, and you lose much of the greatness; and join them, and you infallibly lose the clearness." This is altogether a mistake. The images are vivid enough to make us feel the hovering presence of an awe-inspiring figure having the height and firmness of a tower, and the dusky splendour of a ruined archangel. The poet indicates only that amount of concreteness which is necessary for the clearness of the picture,--only the height and firmness of the tower and the brightness of the sun in eclipse. More concretness would disturb the clearness by calling attention to irrelevant details. To suppose that these images produce the effect because they are crowded and confused (they are crowded and not confused) is to imply that any other images would do equally well, if they were equally crowded. "Separate them, and you lose much of the greatness." Quite true: the image of the tower would want the splendour of the sun. But this much may be said of all descriptions which proceed upon details. And so far from the impressive clearness of the picture vanishing in the crowd of images, it is by these images that the clearness is produced: the details make it impressive, and affect our imagination.

It should be added that Burke came very near a true explanation in the following passage:—"It is difficult to conceive how words can move the passions which belong to real objects without representing these objects clearly. This is difficult to us because we do not sufficiently distinguish between a clear expression and a strong expression. The former regards the understanding; the latter belongs to the passions. The one describes a thing as it is, the other describes it as it is felt. Now as there is a moving tone of voice, an impassioned countenance, an agitated gesture, which affect independently of the things about which they are exerted, so there are words and certain dispositions of words which being peculiarly devoted to passionate subjects, and always used by those who are under the influence of passion, touch and move us more than those which far more clearly and distinctly express the subject-matter." Burke here fails to see that the tones, looks, and gestures are the intelligible symbols of passion—the "images' in the true sense just as words are the intelligible symbols of ideas. The subject-matter is as clearly expressed by the one as by the other; for if the description of a Lion be conveyed in the symbols of admiration or of terror, the subject-matter is THEN a Lion passionately and not zoologically considered. And this Burke himself was led to admit, for he adds, "We yield to sympathy what we refuse to description. The truth is, all verbal description, merely as naked description, though never so exact, conveys so poor and insufficient an idea of the thing described, that it could scarcely have the smallest eflfect if the speaker did not call in to his aid those modes of speech that work a strong and lively feeling in himself. Then, by the contagion of our passions, we catch a fire already kindled in another." This is very true, and it sets clearly forth the fact that naked description, addressed to the calm understanding, has a different subject-matter from description addressed to the feelings, and the symbols by which it is made intelligible must likewise differ. But this in no way impugns the principle of Vision. Intelligible symbols (clear images) are as necessary in the one case as in the other.

IV.

By reducing imagination to the power of forming images, and by insisting that no image can be formed except out of the elements furnished by experience, I do not mean to confound imagination with memory; indeed, the frequent occurrence of great strength of memory with comparative feebleness of imagination, would suffice to warn us against such a conclusion.

Its specific character, that which marks it off from simple memory, is its tendency to selection, abstraction, and recombination. Memory, as passive, simply recalls previous experiences of objects and emotions; from these, imagination, as an active faculty, selects the elements which vividly symbolise the objects or emotions, and either by a process of abstraction allows these to do duty for the whole, or else by a process of recombination creates new objects and new relations in which the objects stand to us or to each other (INVENTION), and the result is an image of great vividness, which has perhaps no corresponding reality in the external world.

Minds differ in the vividness with which they recall the elements of previous experience, and mentally see the absent objects; they differ also in the aptitudes for selection, abstraction, and recombination: the fine selective instinct of the artist, which makes him fasten upon the details which will most powerfully affect us, without any disturbance of the harmony of the general impression, does not depend solely upon the vividness of his memory and the clearness with which the objects are seen, but depends also upon very complex and peculiar conditions of sympathy which we call genius. Hence we find one man remembering a multitude of details, with a memory so vivid that it almost amounts at times to hallucination, yet without any artistic power; and we may find men—Blake was one—with an imagination of unusual activity, who are nevertheless incapable, from deficient sympathy, of seizing upon those symbols which will most affect us. Our native susceptibilities and acquired tastes determine which of the many qualities in an object shall most impress us, and be most clearly recalled. One man remembers the combustible properties of a substance, which to another is memorable for its polarising property; to one man a stream is so much water-power, to another a rendezveus for lovers.

In the close of the last paragraph we came face to face with the great difficulty which constantly arrests speculation on these matters—the existence of special aptitudes vaguely characterised as genius. These are obviously incommunicable. No recipe can be given for genius. No man can be taught how to exercise the power of imagination. But he can be taught how to aid it, and how to assure himself whether he is using it or not. Having once laid hold of the Principle of Vision as a fundamental principle of

Art, he can always thus far apply it, that he can assure himself whether he does or does not distinctly see the cottage he is describing, the rivulet that is gurgling through his verses, or the character he is painting; he can assure himself whether he hears the voice of the speakers, and feels that what they say is true to their natures; he can assure himself whether he sees, as in actual experience, the emotion he is depicting; and he will know that if he does not see these things he must wait until he can, or he will paint them ineffectively. With distinct Vision he will be able to make the best use of his powers of expression; and the most splendid powers of expression will not avail him if his Vision be indistinct. This is true of objects that never were seen by the eye, that never could be seen. It is as true of what are called the highest flights of imagination as of the lowest flights. The mind must SEE the angel or the demon, the hippogriff or centaur, the pixie or the mermaid.

Ruskin notices how repeatedly Turner,—the most imaginative of landscape painters,—introduced into his pictures, after a lapse of many years, memories of something which, however small and unimportant, had struck him in his earlier studies. He believes that all Turner's "composition" was an arrangement of remembrances summoned just as they were wanted, and each in its fittest place. His vision was primarily composed of strong memory of the place itself, and secondarily of memories of other places associated in a harmonious, helpful way with the now central thought. He recalled and selected.

I am prepared to hear of many readers, especially young readers, protesting against the doctrine of this chapter as prosaic. They have been so long accustomed to consider imagination as peculiarly distinguished by its disdain of reality, and Invention as only admirable when its products are not simply new by selection and arrangement, but new in material, that they will reject the idea of involuntary remembrance of something originally experienced as the basis of all Art. Ruskin says of great artists, "Imagine all that any of these men had seen or heard in the whole course of their lives, laid up accurately in their memories as in vast storehouses, extending with the poets even to the slightest intonations of syllables heard in the beginning of their lives, and with painters down to minute folds of drapery and shapes of leaves and stones; and over all this unindexed and immeasurable mass of treasure, the imagination brooding and wandering, but dream-gifted, so as to summon at any moment exactly such a group of ideas as shall justly fit each other." This is the explanation of their genius, as far as it can be explained.

Genius is rarely able to give any account of its own processes. But those who have had ample opportunities of intimately knowing the growth of works in the minds of artists, will bear me out in saying that a vivid memory supplies the elements from a thousand different sources, most of which are quite beyond the power of localisation, the experience of yesterday being strangely intermingled with the dim suggestions of early years, the tones heard in childhood sounding through the diapason of sorrowing maturity; and all these kaleidoscopic fragments are recomposed into images that seem to have a corresponding reality of their own.

As all Art depends on Vision, so the different kinds of Art depend on the different ways in which minds look at things. The painter can only put into his pictures what he sees in Nature; and what he sees will be different from what another sees. A poetical mind sees noble and affecting suggestions in details which the prosaic mind will interpret prosaically. And the true meaning of Idealism is precisely this vision of realities in their highest and most affecting forms, not in the vision of something removed from or opposed to realities. Titian's grand picture of "Peter the Martyr" is, perhaps, as instructive an example as could be chosen of successful Idealism; because in it we have a marvellous presentation of reality as seen by a poetic mind. The figure of the flying monk might have been equally real if it had been an ignoble presentation of terror—the superb tree, which may almost be called an actor in the drama, might have been painted with even greater minuteness, though not perhaps with equal effect upon us, if it had arrested our attention by its details—the dying martyr and the noble assassin might have been made equally real in more vulgar types—but the triumph achieved by Titian is that the mind is filled with a vision of poetic beauty which is felt to be real. An equivalent reality, without the ennobling beauty, would have made the picture a fine piece of realistic art. It is because of this poetic way of seeing things that one painter will give a faithful representation of a very common scene which shall nevertheless affect all sensitive minds as ideal, whereas another painter will represent the same with no greater fidelity, but with a complete absence of poetry. The greater the fidelity, the greater will be the merit of each representation; for if a man pretends to represent an object, he pretends to represent it accurately: the only difference is what the poetical or prosaic mind sees in the object.

Of late years there has been a reaction against conventionalism which called itself Idealism, in favour of DETAILISM which calls itself Realism. As a reaction it has been of service; but it has led to much false criticism, and not a little false art, by an obtrusiveness of Detail and a preference for the Familiar, under the misleading notion of adherence to Nature. If the words Nature and Natural could be entirely banished from language about Art there would be some chance of coming to a rational philosophy of the subject; at present the excessive vagueness and shiftiness of these terms cover any amount of sophism. The pots and pans of Teniers and Van Mieris are natural; the passions and humours of Shakspeare and Moliere are natural; the angels of Fra Angelico and Luini are natural; the

Sleeping Fawn and Fates of Phidias are natural; the cows and misty marshes of Cuyp and the vacillations of Hamlet are equally natural. In fact the natural means TRUTH OF KIND. Each kind of character, each kind of representation, must be judged by itself. Whereas the vulgar error of criticism is to judge of one kind by another, and generally to judge the higher by the lower, to remonstrate with Hamlet for not having the speech and manner of Mr. Jones, to wish that Fra Angelico could have seen with the eyes of the Carracci, to wish verse had been prose, and that ideal tragedy were acted with the easy manner acceptable in drawing-rooms.

The rage for "realism," which is healthy in as far as it insists on truth, has become unhealthy, in as far as it confounds truth with familiarity, and predominance of unessential details. There are other truths besides coats and waistcoats, pots and pans, drawlng-rooms and suburban villas. Life has other aims besides these which occupy the conversation of "Society." And the painter who devotes years to a work representing modern life, yet calls for even more attention to a waistcoat than to the face of a philosopher, may exhibit truth of detail which will delight the tailor-mind, but he is defective in artistic truth, because he ought to be representing something higher than waistcoats, and because our thoughts on modern life fall very casually and without emphasis on waistcoats. In Piloty's much-admired picture of the "Death of Wallenstein" (at Munich), the truth with which the carpet, the velvet, and all other accessories are painted, is certainly remarkable; but the falsehood of giving prominence to such details in a picture representing the dead Wallenstein—as if they were the objects which could possibly arrest our attention and excite our sympathies in such a spectacle—is a falsehood of the realistic school. If a man means to paint upholstery, by all means let him paint it so as to delight and deceive an upholsterer; but if he means to paint a human tragedy, the upholsterer must be subordinate, and velvet must not draw our eyes away from faces.

I have digressed a little from my straight route because I wish to guard the Principle of Vision from certain misconceptions which might arise on a simple statement of it. The principle insists on the artist assuring himself that he distinctly sees what he attempts to represent. WHAT he sees, and HOW he represents it, depend on other principles. To make even this principle of Vision thoroughly intelligible in its application to all forms of Literature and Art, it must be considered in connection with the two other principles—Sincerity and Beauty, which are involved in all successful works. In the next chapter we shall treat of Sincerity.

❋❋❋

Chapter 10
The Principle of Sincerity.

It is always understood as an expression of condemnation when anything in Literature or Art is said to be done for effect; and yet to produce an effect is the aim and end of both.

There is nothing beyond a verbal ambiguity here if we look at it closely, and yet there is a corresponding uncertainty in the conception of Literature and Art commonly entertained, which leads many writers and many critics into the belief that what are called "effects" should be sought, and when found must succeed. It is desirable to clear up this moral ambiguity, as I may call it, and to show that the real method of securing the legitimate effect is not to aim at it, but to aim at the truth, relying on that for securing effect. The condemnation of whatever is "done for effect" obviously springs from indignation at a disclosed insincerity in the artist, who is self-convicted of having neglected truth for the sake of our applause; and we refuse our applause to the flatterer, or give it contemptuously as to a mountebank whose dexterity has amused us.

It is unhappily true that much insincere Literature and Art, executed solely with a view to effect, does succeed by deceiving the public. But this is only because the simulation of truth or the blindness of the public conceals the insincerity. As a maxim, the Principle of Sincerity is admitted. Nothing but what is true, or is held to be true, can succeed; anything which looks like insincerity is condemned. In this respect we may compare it with the maxim of Honesty the best policy. No far-reaching intellect fails to perceive that if all men were uniformly upright and truthful, Life would be more victorious, and Literature more noble. We find, however, both in Life and Literature, a practical disregard of the truth of these propositions almost equivalent to a disbelief in them. Many men are keenly alive to the social advantages of honesty—in the practice of others. They are also strongly impressed with the conviction that in their own particular case the advantage will sometimes lie in not strictly adhering to the rule. Honesty is doubtless the best policy in the long run; but somehow the run here seems so very long, and a short-cut opens such allurements to impatient desire. It requires a firm calm insight, or a noble habit of thought, to steady the wavering mind, and direct it away from delusive short-cuts: to make belief practice, and forego immediate triumph. Many of those who unhesitatingly admit Sincerity to be one great condition of success in Literature find it difficult, and often impossible, to resist the temptation of an insincerity which promises immediate advantage. It is not only the grocers who sand their sugar before prayers. Writers who know well enough that the triumph of falsehood is an unholy triumph, are not deterred from falsehood by that knowledge. They know, perhaps, that, even if undetected, it will press on their own consciences; but the knowledge avails them little. The immediate pressure of the temptation is yielded to, and Sincerity remains a text to be preached to others. To gain applause they will misstate facts, to gain victory in argument they will misrepresent the opinions they oppose; and they suppress the rising misgivings by the dangerous sophism that to discredit error is good work, and by the hope that no one will detect the means by which the work is effected. The saddest aspect of this procedure is that in Literature, as in Life, a temporary success often does reward dishonesty. It would be insincere to conceal it. To gain a reputation as discoverers men will invent or suppress facts. To appear learned they will array their writings in the ostentation of borrowed citations. To solicit the "sweet voices" of the crowd they will feign sentiments they do not feel, and utter what they think the crowd will wish to hear, keeping back whatever the crowd will hear with disapproval. And, as I said, such men often succeed for a time; the fact is so, and we must not pretend that it is otherwise. But it no more disturbs the fundamental truth of the Principle of Sincerity, than the perturbations in the orbit of Mars disturb the truth of Kepler's law.

It is impossible to deny that dishonest men often grow rich and famous, becoming powerful in their parish or in parliament. Their portraits simper from shop windows; and they live and die respected. This success is theirs; yet it is not the success which a noble soul will envy. Apart from the risk of discovery and infamy, there is the certainty of a conscience ill at ease, or if at ease, so blunted in its sensibilities, so given over to lower lusts, that a healthy instinct recoils from such a state. Observe, moreover, that in Literature the possible rewards of dishonesty are small, and the probability of detection great. In Life a dishonest man is chiefly moved by desires towards some tangible result of money or power; if he get these he has got all. The man of letters has a higher aim: the very object of his toil is to secure the sympathy and respect of men; and the rewards of his toil may be paid in money, fame, or consciousness of earnest effort. The first of these may sometimes be gained without Sincerity. Fame may also, for a time, be erected on an unstable ground, though it will inevitably be destroyed again. But the last and not least reward is to be gained by every one without fear of failure, without risk of change. Sincere work is good work, be it never so humble; and sincere work is not only an indestructible delight to the worker by its very genuineness, but is immortal in the best sense, for it lives for ever in its influence. There is no good Dictionary, not even a good Index, that is not in this sense priceless, for it has honestly furthered the work of the world, saving labour to others, setting an example to successors.

Whether I make a careful Index, or an inaccurate one, will probably in no respect affect the money-payment I shall receive. My sins will never fall heavily on me; my virtue will gain me neither extra pence nor praise. I shall be hidden by obscurity from the indignation of those whose valuable time is wasted over my pretence at accuracy, as from the silent gratitude of those whose time is saved by my honest fidelity. The consciousness of faithfulness even to the poor index maker may be a better reward than pence or praise; but of course we cannot expect the unconscientious to believe this. If I sand my sugar, and tell lies over my counter, I may gain the rewards of dishonesty, or I may be overtaken by its Nemesis. But if I am faithful in my work the reward cannot be withheld from me. The obscure workers who, knowing that they will never earn renown yet feel an honourable pride in doing their work faithfully, may be likened to the benevolent who feel a noble delight in performing generous actions which will never be known to be theirs, the only end they seek in such actions being the good which is wrought for others, and their delight being the sympathy with others.

I should be ashamed to insist on truths so little likely to be disputed, did they not point directly at the great source of bad Literature, which, as was said in our first chapter, springs from a want of proper moral guidance rather than from deficiency of talent. The Principle of Sincerity comprises all those qualities of courage, patience, honesty, and simplicity which give momentum to talent, and determine successful Literature. It is not enough to have the eye to see; there must also be the courage to express what the eye has seen, and the steadfastness of a trust in truth. Insight, imagination, grace of style are potent; but their power is delusive unless sincerely guided. If any one should object that this is a truism, the answer is ready: Writers disregard its truth, as traders disregard the truism of honesty being the best policy. Nay, as even the most upright men are occasionally liable to swerve from the truth, so the most upright authors will in some passages desert a perfect sincerity; yet the ideal of both is rigorous truth. Men who are never flagrantly dishonest are at times unveracious in small matters, colouring or suppressing facts with a conscious purpose; and writers who never stole an idea nor pretended to honours for which they had not striven, may be found lapsing into small insincerities, speaking a language which is not theirs, uttering opinions which they expect to gain applause rather than the opinions really believed by them. But if few men are perfectly and persistently sincere, Sincerity is nevertheless the only enduring strength.

The principle is universal, stretching from the highest purposes of Literature down to its smallest details. It underlies the labour of the philosopher, the investigator, the moralist, the poet, the novelist, the critic, the historian, and the compiler. It is visible in the publication of opinions, in the structure of sentences, and in the fidelity of citations. Men utter insincere thoughts, they express themselves in echoes and affectations, and they are careless or dishonest in their use of the labours of others, all the time believing in the virtue of sincerity, all the time trying to make others believe honesty to be the best policy.

Let us glance for a moment at the most important applications of the principle. A man must be himself convinced if he is to convince others. The prophet must be his own disciple, or he will make none. Enthusiasm is contagious: belief creates belief. There is no influence issuing from unbelief or from languid acquiescence. This is peculiarly noticeable in Art, because Art depends on sympathy for its influence, and unless the artist has felt the emotions he depicts we remain unmoved: in proportion to the depth of his feeling is our sympathetic response; in proportion to the shallowness or falsehood of his presentation is our coldness or indifference. Many writers who have been fond of quoting the SI VIS ME FLERE of Horace have written as if they did not believe a word of it; for they have been silent on their own convictions, suppressed their own experience, and falsified their own feelings to repeat the convictions and fine phrases of another. I am sorry that my experience assures me that many of those who will read with complete assent all here written respecting the power of Sincerity, will basely desert their allegiance to the truth the next time they begin to write; and they will desert it because their misguided views of Literature prompt them to think more of what the public is likely to applaud than of what is worth applause; unfortunately for them their estimation of this likelihood is generally based on a very erroneous assumption of public wants: they grossly mistake the taste they pander to.

In all sincere speech there is power, not necessarily great power, but as much as the speaker is capable of. Speak for yourself and from yourself, or be silent. It can be of no good that you should tell in your "clever" feeble way what another has already told us with the dynamic energy of conviction. If you can tell us something that your own eyes have seen, your own mind has thought, your own heart has felt, you will have power over us, and all the real power that is possible for you. If what you have seen is trivial, if what you have thought is erroneous, if what you have felt is feeble, it would assuredly be better that you should not speak at all; but if you insist on speaking Sincerity will secure the uttermost of power.

The delusions of self-love cannot be prevented, but intellectual misconceptions as to the means of achieving success may be corrected. Thus although it may not be possible for any introspection to discover whether we have genius or effective power, it is quite possible to know whether we are trading upon borrowed capital, and whether the eagle's feathers have been picked up by us, or grow from our own wings. I hear some one of my young readers exclaim against the disheartening tendency of what is here said. Ambitious of success, and conscious that he has no great resources within his own experience, he shrinks from the idea of being thrown upon his naked faculty and limited resources, when he feels himself capable of dexterously using the resources of others, and so producing an effective work. "Why," he asks, "must I confine myself to my own small experience, when I feel persuaded that it will interest no one? Why express the opinions to which my own investigations have led me when I suspect that they are incomplete, perhaps altogether erroneous, and when I know that they will not be popular because they are unlike those which have hitherto found favour? Your restrictions would reduce two-thirds of our writers to silence!"

This reduction would, I suspect, be welcomed by every one except the gagged writers; but as the idea of its being operative is too chimerical for us to entertain it, and as the purpose of these pages is to expound the principles of success and failure, not to make Quixotic onslaughts on the windmills of stupidity and conceit, I answer my young interrogator: "Take warning and do not write. Unless you believe in yourself, only noodles will believe in you, and they but tepidly. If your experience seems trivial to you, it must seem trivial to us. If your thoughts are not fervid convictions, or sincere doubts, they will not have the power of convictions and doubts. To believe in yourself is the first step; to proclaim your belief the next. You cannot assume the power of another. No jay becomes an eagle by borrowing a few eagle feathers. It is true that your sincerity will not be a guarantee of power. You may believe that to be important and novel which we all recognise as trivial and old. You may be a madman, and believe yourself a prophet. You may be a mere echo, and believe yourself a voice. These are among the delusions against which none of us are protected. But if Sincerity is not necessarily a guarantee of power, it is a necessary condition of power, and no genius or prophet can exist without it."

"The highest merit we ascribe to Moses, Plato, and Milton," says Emerson, "is that they set at nought books and traditions, and spoke not what men thought, but what they thought. A man should learn to detect and watch that gleam of light which flashes across his mind from within; more than the lustre of the firmament of bards and sages. Yet he dismisses without notice his thought because it is his. In every work of genius we recognise our own rejected thoughts; they come back to us with a certain alienated majesty." It is strange that any one who has recognised the individuality of all works of lasting influence, should not also recognise the fact that his own individuality ought to be steadfastly preserved. As Emerson says in continuation, "Great works of art have no more affecting lesson for us than this. They teach us to abide by our spontaneous impressions with good-humoured inflexibility, then most when the whole cry of voices is on the other side. Else tomorrow a stranger will say with masterly good sense, precisely what we have thought and felt all the time, and we shall be forced to take with shame our opinion from another." Accepting the opinions of another and the tastes of another is very different from agreement in opinion and taste. Originality is independence, not rebellion; it is sincerity, not antagonism. Whatever you believe to be true and false, that proclaim to be true and false; whatever you think admirable and beautiful, that should be your model, even if all your friends and all the critics storm at you as a crochet-monger and an eccentric. Whether the public will feel its truth and beauty at once, or after long years, or never cease to regard it as paradox and ugliness, no man can foresee; enough for you to know that you have done your best, have been true to yourself, and that the utmost power inherent in your work has been displayed.

An orator whose purpose is to persuade men must speak the things they wish to hear; an orator, whose purpose is to move men, must also avoid disturbing the emotional effect by any obtrusion of intellectual antagonism; but an author whose purpose is to instruct men, who appeals to the intellect, must be careless of their opinions, and think only of truth. It will often be a question when a man is or is not wise in advancing unpalateable opinions, or in preaching heresies; but it can never be a question that a man should be silent if unprepared to speak the truth as he conceives it. Deference to popular opinion is one great source of bad writing, and is all the more disastrous because the deference is paid to some purely hypothetical requirement. When a man fails to see the truth of certain generally accepted views, there is no law compelling him to provoke animosity by announcing his dissent. He may be excused if he shrink from the lurid glory of martyrdom; he may be justified in not placing himself in a position of singularity. He may even be commended for not helping to perplex mankind with doubts which he feels to be founded on limited and possibly erroneous investigation. But if allegiance to truth lays no stern command upon him to speak out his immature dissent, it does lay a stern command not to speak out hypocritical assent.

There are many justifications of silence; there can be none of insincerity.

Nor is this less true of minor questions; it applies equally to opinions on matters of taste and personal feeling. Why should I echo what seem to me the extravagant praises of Raphael's "Transfiguration," when, in truth, I do not greatly admire that famous work ? There is no necessity for me to speak on the subject at all; but if I do speak, surely it is to utter my impressions, and not to repeat what others have uttered. Here, then, is a dilemma; if I say what I really feel about this work, after vainly endeavouring day after day to discover the transcendent merits discovered by thousands (or at least proclaimed by them), there is every likelihood of my incurring the contempt of connoisseurs, and of being reproached with want of taste in art. This is the bugbear which scares thousands. For myself, I would rather incur the contempt of connoisseurs than my own; the repreach of defective taste is more endurable than the reproach of insincerity. Suppose I am deficient in the requisite knowledge and sensibility, shall I be less so by pretending to admire what really gives me no exquisite enjoyment? Will the pleasure I feel in pictures be enhanced because other men consider me right in my admlration, or diminished because they consider me wrong?

[I have never thoroughly understood the painful anxiety of people to be shielded against the dishonouring suspicion of not rightly appreciating pictures, even when the very phrases they use betray their ignorance and insensibility. Many will avow their indifference to music, and almost boast of their ignorance of science; will sneer at abstract theories, and profess the most tepid interest in history, who would feel it an unpardonable insult if you doubted their enthusiasm for painting and the "old masters" (by them secretly identified with the brown masters). It is an insincerity fostered by general pretence. Each man is afraid to declare his real sentiments in the presence of others equally timid. Massive authority overawes genuine feeling].

The opinion of the majority is not lightly to be rejected; but neither is it to be carelessly echoed. There is something noble in the submission to a great renown, which makes all reverence a healthy attitude if it be genuine. When I think of the immense fame of Raphael, and of how many high and delicate minds have found exquisite delight even in the "Transfiguration," and especially when I recall how others of his works have affected me, it is natural to feel some diffidence in opposing the judgment of men whose studies have given them the best means of forming that judgment—a diffidence which may keep me silent on the matter. To start with the assumption that you are right, and all who oppose you are fools, cannot be a safe method. Nor in spite of a conviction that much of the admiration expressed for the "Transfiguration" is lip-homage and tradition, ought the non-admiring to assume that all of it is insincere. It is quite compatible with modesty to be perfectly independent, and with sincerity to be respectful to the opinions and tastes of others. If you express any opinion, you are bound to express your real opinion; let critics and admirers utter what dithyrambs they please. Were this terror of not being thought correct in taste once got rid of, how many stereotyped judgments on books and pictures would be broken up! and the result of this sincerity would be some really valuable criticism. In the presence of Raphael's "Sistine Madonna," Titian's "Peter the Martyr," or Masaccio's great frescoes in the Brancacci Chapel, one feels as if there had been nothing written about these mighty works, so little does any eulogy discriminate the elements of their profound effects, so little have critics expressed their own thoughts and feelings. Yet every day some wandering connoisseur stands before these pictures, and at once, without waiting to let them sink deep into his mind, discovers all the merits which are stereotyped in the criticisms, and discovers nothing else. He does not wait to feel, he is impatient to range himself with men of taste; he discards all genuine impressions, replacing them with vague conceptions of what he is expected to see.

Inasmuch as Success must be determined by the relation between the work and the public, the sincerity which leads a man into open revolt against established opinions may seem to be an obstacle. Indeed, publishers, critics, and friends are always loud in their prophecies against originality and independence on this very ground; they do their utmost to stifle every attempt at novelty, because they fix their eyes upon a hypothetical public taste, and think that only what has already been proved successful can again succeed; forgetting that whatever has once been done need not be done over again, and forgetting that what is now commonplace was once originality. There are cases in which a disregard of public opinion will inevitably call forth opprobrium or neglect; but there is no case in which Sincerity is not strength. If I advance new views in Philosophy or Theology, I cannot expect to have many adherents among minds altogether unprepared for such views; yet it is certain that even those who most fiercely oppose me will recognise the power of my voice if it is not a mere echo; and the very novelty will challenge attention, and at last gain adherents if my views have any real insight. At any rate the point to be considered is this, that whether the novel views excite opposition or applause, the one condition of their success is that they be believed in by the propagator. The public can only be really moved by what is genuine. Even an error if believed in will have greater force than an insincere truth. Lip-advocacy only rouses lip-homage. It is belief which gives momentum.

Nor is it any serious objection to what is here said, that insincerity and timid acquiescence in the opinion and tastes of thc public do often gain applause and temporary success. Sanding the sugar is not immediately unprofitable. There is an unpleasant popularity given to falsehood in this world of ours; but we love the truth notwithstanding, and with a more enduring love. Who does not know what it is to listen to public speakers pouring forth expressions of hollow belief and sham enthusiasm, snatching at commonplaces with a fervour as of faith, emphasising insincerities as if to make up by emphasis what is wanting in feeling, all the while saying not only what they do not believe, but what the listeners KNOW they do not believe, and what the listeners, though they roar assent, do not themselves believe—a turbulence of sham, the very noise of which stuns the conscience? Is such an orator really enviable, although thunders of applause may have greeted his efforts? Is that success, although the newspapers all over the kingdom may be reporting the speech? What influence remains when the noise of the shouts has died away? Whereas, if on the same occasion one man gave utterance to a sincere thought, even if it were not a very wise thought, although the silence of the public—perhaps its hisses—may have produced an impression of failure, yet there is success, for the thought will re-appear and mingle with the thoughts of men to be adopted or combated by them, and may perhaps in a few years mark out the speaker as a man better worth listening to than the noisy orator whose insincerity was so much cheered.

The same observation applies to books. An author who waits upon the times, and utters only what he thinks the world will like to hear, who sails with the stream, admiring everything which it is "correct taste" to admire, despising everything which has not yet received that Hall-mark, sneering at the thoughts of a great thinker not yet accepted as such, and slavishly repeating the small phrases of a thinker who has gained renown, flippant and contemptuous towards opinions which he has not taken the trouble to understand, and never venturing to oppose even the errors of men in authority, such an author may indeed by dint of a certain dexterity in assorting the mere husks of opinion gain the applause of reviewers, who will call him a thinker, and of indolent men and women who will pronounce him "so clever ;" but triumphs of this kind are like oratorical triumphs after dinner. Every autumn the earth is strewed with the dead leaves of such vernal successes.

I would not have the reader conclude that because I advocate plain-speaking even of unpopular views, I mean to imply that originality and sincerity are always in opposition to public opinion. There are many points both of doctrine and feeling in which the world is not likely to be wrong. But in all cases it is desirable that men should not pretend to believe opinions which they really reject, or express emotions they do not feel. And this rule is universal. Even truthful and modest men will sometimes violate the rule under the mistaken idea of being eloquent by means of the diction of eloquence. This is a source of bad Literature. There are certain views in Religion, Ethics, and Politics, which readily lend themselves to eloquence, because eloquent men have written largely on them, and the temptation to secure this facile effect often seduces men to advocate these views in preference to views they really see to be more rational. That this eloquence at second-hand is but feeble in its effect, does not restrain others from repeating it. Experience never seems to teach them that grand speech comes only from grand thoughts, passionate speech from passionate emotions. The pomp and roll of words, the trick of phrase, the rhytlnn and the gesture of an orator, may all be imitated, but not his eloquence. No man was ever eloquent by trying to be eloquent, but only by being so. Trying leads to the vice of "fine writing" – the plague-spot of Literature, not only unhealthy in itself, and vulgarising the grand language which should be reserved for great thoughts, but encouraging that tendency to select only those views upon which a spurious enthusiasm can most readily graft the representative abstractions and stirring suggestions which will move public applause. The "fine writer" will always prefer the opinion which is striking to the opinion which is true. He frames his sentences by the ear, and is only dissatisfied with them when their cadences are ill-distributed, or their diction is too familiar. It seldom occurs to him that a sentence should accurately express his meaning and no more; indeed there is not often a definite meaning to be expressed, for the thought which arose vanished while he tried to express it, and the sentence, instead of being determined by and moulded on a thought, is determined by some verbal suggestion. Open any book or periodical, and see how frequently the writer does not, cannot, mean what he says; and you will observe that in general the defect does not arise from any poverty in our language, but from the habitual carelessness which allows expressions to be written down unchallenged provided they are sufficiently harmonious, and not glaringly inadequate.

The slapdash insincerity of modern style entirely sets at nought the first principle of writing, which is accuracy. The art of writing is not, as many seem to imagine, the art of bringing fine phrases into rhythmical order, but the art of placing before the reader intelligible symbols of the thoughts and feelings in the writer's mind. Endeavour to be faithful, and if there is any beauty in your thought, your style will be beautiful; if there is any real emotion to express, the expression will be moving. Never rouge your style. Trust to your native pallor rather than to cosmetics. Try to make us see what you see and to feel what you feel, and banish from your mind whatever phrases others may have used to express what was in their thoughts, but is not in yours. Have you never observed what a light impression writers have produced, in spite of a profusion of images, antitheses, witty epigrams, and rolling periods, whereas some simpler style, altogether wanting in such "brilliant passage," has gained the attention and respect of thousands? Whatever is stuck on as ornament affects us as ornament; we do not think an old hag young and handsome because the jewels flash from her brow and bosom; if we envy her wealth, we do not admire her beauty.

What "fine writing" is to prosaists, insincere imagery is to poets: it is introduced for effect, not used as expression. To the real poet an image comes spontaneously, or if it comes as an afterthought, it is chosen because it expresses his meaning and helps to paint the picture which is in his mind, not because it is beautiful in itself. It is a symbol, not an ornament. Whether the image rise slowly before the mind during contemplation, or is seen in the same flash which discloses the picture, in each case it arises by natural association, and is SEEN, not SOUGHT. The inferior poet is dissatisfied with what he sees, and casts about in search after something more striking. He does not wait till an image is borne in upon the tide of memory, he seeks for an image that will be picturesque; and being without the delicate selective instinct which guides the fine artist, he generally chooses something which we feel to be not exactly in its right place. He thus—

"With gold and silver covers every part,
And hides with ornament his want of art."

Be true to your own soul, and do not try to express the thought of another. "If some people," says Ruskin, "really see angels where others see only empty space, let them paint angels: only let not anybody else think they can paint an angel too, on any calculated principles of the angelic." Unhappily this is precisely what so many will attempt, inspired by the success of the angelic painter. Nor will the failure of others warn them.

Whatever is sincerely felt or believed, whatever forms part of the imaginative experience, and is not simply imitation or hearsay, may fitly be given to the world, and will always maintain an infinite superiority over imitative splendour; because although it by no means follows that whatever has formed part of the artist's experience must be impressive, or can do without artistic presentation, yet his artistic power will always be greater over his own material than over another's. Emerson has well remarked "that those facts, words, persons which dwell in a man's memory without his being able to say why, remain because they have a relation to him not less real for being as yet unapprehended. They are symbols of value to him as they can interpret parts of his consciousness which he would vainly seek words for in the conventional images of books and other minds. What attracts my attention shall have it; as I will go to the man who knocks at my door while a thousand persons as worthy go by it to whom I give no regard. It is enough that these particulars speak to me. A few anecdotes, a few traits of character, manners, faces, a few incidents have an emphasis in your memory out of all proportion to their apparent significance if you measure them by ordinary standards. They relate to your gift. Let them have their weight, and do not reject them, or cast about for illustrations and facts more usual in literature."

In the notes to the last edition of his poems, Wordsworth specified the particular occasions which furnished him with particular images. It was the things he had SEEN which he put into his verses; and that is why they affect us. It matters little whether the poet draws his images directly from present experience, or indirectly from memory—whether the sight of the slow-sailing swan, that "floats double swan and shadow" be at once transferred to the scene of the poem he is writing, or come back upon him in after years to complete some picture in his mind; enough that the image be suggested, and not sought.

The sentence from Ruskin, quoted just now, will guard against the misconception that a writer, because told to rely on his own experience, is enjoined to forego the glory and delight of creation even of fantastic types. He is only told never to pretend to see what he has not seen. He is urged to follow Imagination in her most erratic course, though like a will-o'-wisp she lead over marsh and fen away from the haunts of mortals; but not to pretend that he is following a will-o'-wisp when his vagrant fancy never was allured by one. It is idle to paint fairies and goblins unless you have a genuine vision of them which forces you to paint them. They are poetical objects, but only to poetic minds. "Be a plain photographer if you possibly can," says Ruskin, "if Nature meant you for anything else she will force you to it; but never try to be a prophet; go on quietly with your hard camp work, and the spirit will come to you as it did to Eldad and Medad if you are appointed to it." Yes: if you are appointed to it; if your faculties are such that this high success is possible, it will come, provided the faculties are employed with sincerity. Otherwise it cannot come. No insincere effort can secure it.

If the advice I give to reject every insincerity in writing seem cruel, because it robs the writer of so many of his effects--if it seem disheartening to earnestly warn a man not to TRY to be eloquent, but only to BE eloquent when his thoughts move with an impassioned LARGO—if throwing a writer back upon his naked faculty seem especially distasteful to those who have a painful misgiving that their faculty is small, and that the uttermost of their own power would be far from impressive, my answer is that I have no hope of dissuading feeble writers from the practice of insincerity, but as under no circumstances can they become good writers and achieve success, my analysis has no reference to them, my advice has no aim at them. It is to the young and strong, to the ambitious and the earnest, that my words are addressed. It is to wipe the film from their eyes, and make them see, as they will see directly the truth is placed before them, how easily we are all seduced into greater or less insincerity of thought, of feeling, and of style, either by reliance on other writers, from whom we catch the trick of thought and turn of phrase, or from some preconceived view of what the public will prefer. It is to the young and strong I say: Watch vigilantly every phrase you write, and assure yourself that it expresses what you mean; watch vigilantly every thought you express, and assure yourself that it is yours, not another's; you may share it with another, but you must not adopt it from him for the nonce. Of course, if you are writing humorously or dramatically, you will not be expected to write your own serious opinions. Humour may take its utmost licence, yet be sincere. The dramatic genius may incarnate itself in a hundred shapes, yet in each it will speak what it feels to be the truth. If you are imaginatively representing the feelings of another, as in some playful exaggeration or some dramatic personation, the truth required of you is imaginative truth, not your personal views and feelings. But when you write in your own person you must be rigidly veracious, neither pretending to admire what you do not admire, or to despise what in secret you rather like, nor surcharging your admiration and enthusiasm to bring you into unison with the public chorus. This vigilance may render Literature more laborious; but no one ever supposed that success was to be had on easy terms; and if you only write one sincere page where you might have written twenty insincere pages, the one page is worth writing—it is Literature.

Sincerity is not only effective and honourable, it is also much less difficult than is commonly supposed. To take a trifling example: If for some reason I cannot, or do not, choose to verify a quotation which may be useful to my purpose, what is to prevent my saying that the quotation is taken at second-hand? It is true, if my quotations are for the most part second-hand and are acknowledged as such, my erudition will appear scanty. But it will only appear what it is. Why should I pretend to an erudition which is not mine? Sincerity forbids it. Prudence whispers that the pretence is, after all, vain, because those, and those alone, who can rightly estimate erudition will infallibly detect my pretence, whereas those whom I have deceived were not worth deceiving. Yet in spite of Sincerity and Prudence, how shamelessly men compile second-hand references, and display in borrowed footnotes a pretence of labour and of accuracy! I mention this merely to show how, even in the humbler class of compilers, the Principle of Sincerity may find fit illustrations, and how honest work, even in references, belongs to the same category as honest work in philosophy or poetry.

Chapter V
The Principle of Beauty.

It is not enough that a man has clearness of Vision, and reliance on Sincerity, he must also have the art of Expression, or he will remain obscure. Many have had "The visionary eye, the faculty to see the thing that hath been as the thing which is," but either from native defect, or the mistaken bias of education, have been frustrated in the attempt to give their visions beautiful or intelligible shape. The art which could give them shape is doubtless intimately dependent on clearness of eye and sincerity of purpose, but it is also something over and above these, and comes from an organic aptitude not less special, when possessed with fulness, than the aptitude for music or drawing. Any instructed person can write, as any one can learn to draw; but to write well, to express ideas with felicity and force, is not an accomplishment but a talent. The power of seizing unapparent relations of things is not always conjoined with the power of selecting the fittest verbal symbols by which they can be made apparent to others: the one is the power of the thinker, the other the power of the writer.

"Style," says De Quincey, "has two separate functions-- first, to brighten the INTELLIGIBILITY of a subject which is obscure to the understanding; secondly, to regenerate the normal POWER and impressiveness of a subject which has become dormant to the sensibilities. . . . . Decaying lineaments are to be retraced and faded colouring to be refreshed." To effect these purposes we require a rich verbal memory from which to select the symbols best fitted to call up images in the reader's mind, and we also require the delicate selective instinct to guide us in the choice and arrangement of those symbols, so that the rhythm and cadence may agreeably attune the mind, rendering it receptive to the impressions meant to be communicated. A copious verbal memory, like a copious memory of facts, is only one source of power, and without the high controlling faculty of the artist may lead to diffusive indecision. Just as one man, gilted with keen insight, will from a small stock of facts extricate unapparent relations to which others, rich in knowledge, have been blind; so will a writer gifted with a fine instinct select from a narrow range of phrases symbols of beauty and of power utterly beyond the reach of commonplace minds. It is often considered, both by writers and readers, that fine language makes fine writers; yet no one supposes that fine colours make a fine painter. The COPIA VERBORUM is often a weakness and a snare. As Arthur Helps says, men use several epithets in the hope that one of them may fit. But the artist knows which epithet does fit, uses that, and rejects the rest. The characteristic weakness of bad writers is inaccuracy: their symbols do not adequately express their ideas. Pause but for a moment over their sentences, and you perceive that they are using language at random, the choice being guided rather by some indistinct association of phrases, or some broken echoes of familiar sounds, than by any selection of words to represent ideas. I read the other day of the truck system being "rampant" in a certain district; and every day we may meet with similar echoes of familiar words which betray the flaccid condition of the writer's mind drooping under the labour of expression.

Except in the rare cases of great dynamic thinkers whose thoughts are as turning-points in the history of our race, it is by Style that writers gain distinction, by Style they secure their immortality. In a lower sphere many are remarked as writers although they may lay no claim to distinction as thinkers, if they have the faculty of felicitously expressing the ideas of others; and many who are really remarkable as thinkers gain but slight recognition from the public, simply because in them the faculty of expression is feeble. In proportion as the work passes from the sphere of passionless intelligence to that of impassioned intelligence, from the region of demonstration to the region of emotion, the art of Style becomes more complex, its necessity more imperious. But even in Philosophy and Science the art is both subtle and necessary; the choice and arrangement of the fitting symbols, though less difficult than in Art, is quite indispensable to success. If the distinction which I formerly drew between the Scientific and the Artistic tendencies be accepted, it will disclose a corresponding difference in the Style which suits a ratiocinative exposition fixing attention on abstract relations, and an emotive exposition fixing attention on objects as related to the feelings. We do not expect the scientific writer to stir our emotions, otherwise than by the secondary influences which arise from our awe and delight at the unveiling of new truths. In his own researches he should extricate himself from the perturbing influences of emotion, and consequently he should protect us from such suggestions in his exposition. Feellng too often smites intellect with blindness, and intellect too often paralyses the free play of emotion, not to call for a decisive separation of the two. But this separation is no ground for the disregard of Style in works, of pure demonstration—as we shall see by-and-by.

The Principle of Beauty is only another name for Style, which is an art, incommunicable as are all other arts, but like them subordinated to laws founded on psychological conditions. The laws constitute the Philosophy of Criticism; and I shall have to ask the reader's indulgence if for the first time I attempt to expound them scientifically in the chapter to which the present is only an introduction. A knowledge of these laws, even presuming them to be accurately expounded, will no more give a writer the power of felicitous expression than a knowledge of the laws of colour, perspective, and proportion will enable a critic to paint a picture. But all good writing must conform to these laws; all bad writing will be found to violate them. And the utility of the knowledge will be that of a constant monitor, warning the artist of the errors into which he has slipped, or into which he may slip if unwarned.

How is it that while every one acknowledges the importance of Style, and numerous critics from Quinctilian and Longinus down to Quarterly Reviewers have written upon it, very little has been done towards a satisfactory establishment of principles? Is it not partly because the critics have seldom held the true purpose of Style steadily before their eyes, and still seldomer justified their canons by deducing them from psychological conditions? To my apprehension they seem to have mistaken the real sources of influence, and have fastened attention upon some accidental or collateral details, instead of tracing the direct connection between effects and causes. Misled by the splendour of some great renown they have concluded that to write like Cicero or to paint like Titian must be the pathway to success; which is true in one sense, and profoundly false as they understand it. One pestilent contagious error issued from this misconception, namely, that all maxims confirmed by the practice of the great artists must be maxims for the art; although a close examination might reveal that the practice of these artists may have been the result of their peculiar individualities or of the state of culture at their epoch. A true Philosophy of Criticism would exhibit in how far such maxims were universal, as founded on laws of human nature, and in how far adaptations to particular individualities. A great talent will discover new methods. A great success ought to put us on the track of new principles. But the fundamental laws of Style, resting on the truths of human nature, may be illustrated, they cannot be guaranteed by any individual success. Moreover, the strong individuality of the artist will create special modifications of the laws to suit himself, making that excellent or endurable which in other hands would be intolerable. If the purpose of Literature be the sincere expression of the individual's own ideas and feelings it is obvious that the cant about the "best models" tends to pervert and obstruct that expression. Unless a man thinks and feels precisely after the manner of Cicero and Titian it is manifestly wrong for him to express himself in their way. He may study in them the principles of effect, and try to surprise some of their secrets, but he should resolutely shun all imitation of them. They ought to be illustrations not authorities, studies not models.

The fallacy about models is seen at once if we ask this simple question: Will the practice of a great writer justify a solecism in grammar or a confusion in logic? No. Then why should it justify any other detail not to be reconciled with universal truth? If we are forced to invoke the arbitration of reason in the one case, we must do so in the other. Unless we set aside the individual practice whenever it is irreconcilable with general principles, we shall be unable to discriminate in a successful work those merits which SECURED from those demerits which ACCOMPANIED success. Now this is precisely the condition in which Criticism has always been. It has been formal instead of being psychological: it has drawn its maxims from the works of successful artists, instead of ascertaining the psychological principles involved in the effects of those works. When the perplexed dramatist called down curses on the man who invented fifth acts, he never thought of escaping from his tribulation by writing a play in four acts; the formal canon which made five acts indispensable to a tragedy was drawn from the practice of great dramatists, but there was no demonstration of any psychological demand on the part of the audience for precisely five acts.

[English critics are much less pedantic in adherence to "rules" than the French, yet when, many years ago, there appeared a tragedy in three acts, and without a death, these innovations were considered inadmissible; and if the success of the work had been such as to elicit critical discussion, the necessity of five acts and a death would doubtless have been generally insisted on].

Although no instructed mind will for a moment doubt the immense advantage of the stimulus and culture derived from a reverent familiarity with the works of our great predecessors and contemperaries, there is a pernicious error which has been fostered by many instructed minds, rising out of their reverence for greatness and their forgetfulness of the ends of Literature. This error is the notion of "models," and of fixed canons drawn from the practice of great artists. It substitutes Imitation for Invention; reproduction of old types instead of the creation of new. There is more bad than good work produced in consequence of the assiduous following of models. And we shall seldom be very wide of the mark if in our estimation of youthful productions we place more reliance on their departures from what has been already done, than on their resemblances to the best artists. An energetic crudity, even a riotous absurdity, has more promise in it than a clever and elegant mediocrity, because it shows that the young man is speaking out of his own heart, and struggling to express himself in his own way rather than in the way he finds in other men's books. The early works of original writers are usually very bad; then succeeds a short interval of imitation in which the influence of some favourite author is distinctly traceable; but this does not last long, the native independence of the mind reasserts itself, and although perhaps academic and critical demands are somewhat disregarded, so that the original writer on account of his very originality receives but slight recognition from the authorities, nevertheless if there is any real power in the voice it soon makes itself felt in the world. There is one word of counsel I would give to young authors, which is that they should be humbly obedient to the truth proclaimed by their own souls, and haughtily indifferent to the remonstrances of critics founded solely on any departure from the truths expressed by others. It by no means follows that because a work is unlike works that have gone before it, therefore it is excellent or even tolerable; it may be original in error or in ugliness; but one thing is certain, that in proportion to its close fidelity to the matter and manner of existing works will be its intrinsic worthlessness. And one of the severest assaults on the fortitude of an unacknowledged writer comes from the knowledge that his critics, with rare exceptions, will judge his work in reference to pre-existing models, and not in reference to the ends of Literature and the laws of human nature. He knows that he will be compared with artists whom he ought not to resemble if his work have truth and originality; and finds himself teased with disparaging remarks which are really compliments in their objections. He can comfort himself by his trust in truth and the sincerity of his own work. He may also draw strength from the reflection that the public and posterity may cordially appreciate the work in which constituted authorities see nothing but failure. The history of Literature abounds in examples of critics being entirely at fault missing the old familiar landmarks, these guides at once set up a shout of warning that the path has been missed.

Very noticeable is the fact that of the thousands who have devoted years to the study of the classics, especially to the "niceties of phrase" and "chastity of composition," so much prized in these classics, very few have learned to write with felicity, and not many with accuracy. Native incompetence has doubtless largely influenced this result in men who are insensible to the nicer shades of distinction in terms, and want the subtle sense of congruity; but the false plan of studying "models" without clearly understanding the psychological conditions which the effects involve, without seeing why great writing is effective, and where it is merely individual expression, has injured even vigorous minds and paralysed the weak. From a similar mistake hundreds have deceived themselves in trying to catch the trick of phrase peculiar tn some distinguished contemporary. In vain do they imitate the Latinisms and antitheses of Johnson, the epigrammatic sentences of Macaulay, the colloquial ease of Thackeray, the cumulative pomp of Milton, the diffusive play of De Quincey: a few friendly or ignorant reviewers may applaud it as "brilliant writing," but the public remains unmoved. It is imitation, and as such it is lifeless.

We see at once the mistake directly we understand that a genuine style is the living body of thought, not a costume that can be put on and off; it is the expression of the writer's mind; it is not less the incarnation of his thoughts in verbal symbols than a picture is the painter's incarnation of his thoughts in symbols of form and colour. A man may, if it please him, dress his thoughts in the tawdry splendour of a masquerade. But this is no more Literature than the masquerade is Life.

No Style can be good that is not slncere. It must be the expression of its author's mind. There are, of course, certain elements of composition which must be mastered as a dancer learns his steps, but the style of the writer, like the grace of the dancer, is only made effective by such mastery; it springs from a deeper source. Initiation into the rules of construction will save us from some gross errors of composltion, but it will not make a style. Still less will imitation of another's manner make one. In our day there are many who imitate Macaulay's short sentences, iterations, antitheses, geographical and historical illustrations, and eighteenth century diction, but who accepts them as Macaulays? They cannot seize the secret of his charm, because that charm lies in the felicity of his talent, not in the structure of his sentences; in the fulness of his knowledge, not in the character of his illustrations. Other men aim at ease and vigour by discarding Latinisms, and admitting colloquialisms; but vigour and ease are not to be had on recipe. No study of models, no attention to rules, will give the easy turn, the graceful phrase, the simple word, the fervid movement, or the large clearness; a picturesque talent will express itself in concrete images; a genial nature will smile in pleasant firms and inuendos; a rapid, unhesitating, imperious mind will deliver its quick incisive phrases; a full deliberating mind will overflow in ample paragraphs laden with the weight of parentheses and qualifying suggestions. The style which is good in one case would be vicious in another. The broken rhythm which increases the energy of one style would ruin the LARGO of another. Both are excellencies where both are natural.

We are always disagreeably impressed by an obvious imitation of the manner of another, because we feel it to be an insincerity, and also because it withdraws our attention from the thing said, to the way of saying it. And here lies the great lesson writers have to learn—namely, that they should think of the immediate purpose of their writing, which is to convey truths and emotions, in symbols and images, intelligible and suggestive. The racket-player keeps his eye on the ball he is to strike, not on the racket with which he strikes. If the writer sees vividly, and will say honestly what he sees, and how he sees it, he may want something of the grace and felicity of other men, but he will have all the strength and felicity with which nature has endowed him. More than that he cannot attain, and he will fall very short of it in snatching at the grace which is another's. Do what he will, he cannot escape from the infirmities of his own mind: the affectation, arrogance, ostentation, hesitation, native in the man will taint his style, no matter how closely he may copy the manner of another. For evil and for good, LE STYLE EST DE L'HOMME MEME.

The French critics, who are singularly servile to all established reputations, and whose unreasoning idolatry of their own classics is one of the reasons why their Literature is not richer, are fond of declaring with magisterial emphasis that the rules of good taste and the canons of style were fixed once and for ever by their great writers in the seventeenth century. The true ambition of every modern is said to be by careful study of these models to approach (though with no hope of equalling) their chastity and elegance. That a writer of the nineteenth century should express himself in the manner which was admirable in the seventeenth is an absurdity which needs only to be stated. It is not worth refuting. But it never presents itself thus to the French. In their minds it is a lingering remnant of that older superstition which believed the Ancients to have discovered all wisdom, so that if we could only surprise the secret of Aristotle's thoughts and clearly comprehend the drift of Plato's theories (which unhappily was not clear) we should compass all knowledge. How long this superstition lasted cannot accurately be settled; perhaps it is not quite extinct even yet; but we know how little the most earnest students succeeded in surprising the secrets of the universe by reading Greek treatises, and how much by studying the universe itself. Advancing Science daily discredits the superstition; yet the advance of Criticism has not yet wholly discredited the parallel superstition in Art. The earliest thinkers are no longer considered the wisest, but the earliest artists are still proclaimed the finest. Even those who do not believe in this superiority are, for the most part, overawed by tradition and dare not openly question the supremacy of works which in their private convictions hold a very subordinate rank. And this reserve is encouraged by the intemperate scorn of those who question the supremacy without having the knowledge or the sympathy which could fairly appreciate the earlier artists. Attacks on the classics by men ignorant of the classical languages tend to perpetuate the superstition.

But be the merit of the classics, ancient and modern, what it may, no writer can become a classic by imitating them. The principle of Sincerity here ministers to the principle of Beauty by forbidding imitation and enforcing rivalry. Write what you can, and if you have the grace of felicitous expression or the power of energetic expression your style will be admirable and admired. At any rate see that it be your own, and not another's; on no other terms will the world listen to it. You cannot be eloquent by borrowing from the opulence of another; you cannot be humorous by mimicking the whims of another; what was a pleasant smile dimpling his features becomes a grimace on yours.

It will not be supposed that I would have the great writers disregardod, as if nothing were to be learned from them; but the study of great writers should be the study of general principles as illustrated or revealed in these writers; and if properly pursued it will of itself lead to a condemnation of the notion of models. What we may learn from them is a nice discrimination of the symbols which intelligibly express the shades of meaning and kindle emotion. The writer wishes to give his thoughts a literary form. This is for others, not for himself; consequently he must, before all things, desire to be intelligible, and to be so he must adapt his expressions to the mental condition of his audience. If he employs arbitrary symbols, such as old words in new and unexpected senses, he may be clear as daylight to himself, but to others, dark as fog. And the difficulty of original writing lies in this, that what is new and individual must find expression in old symbols. This difficulty can only be mastered by a peculiar talent, strengthened and rendered nimble by practice, and the commerce with original minds. Great writers should be our companions if we would learn to write greatly; but no familiarity with their manner will supply the place of native endowment. Writers are born, no less than poets, and like poets, they learn to make their native gifts effective. Practice, aiding their vigilant sensibility, teaches them, perhaps unconsciously, certain methods of effective presentation, how one arrangement of words carries with it more power than another, how familiar and concrete expressions are demanded in one place, and in another place abstract expressions unclogged with disturbing suggestions. Every author thus silently amasses a store of empirical rules, furnished by his own practice, and confirmed by the practice of others. A true Philosophy of Criticism would reduce these empirical rules to science by ranging them under psychological laws, thus demonstrating the validity of the rules, not in virtue of their having been employed by Cicero or Addison, by Burke or Sydney Smith, but in virtue of their conformity with the constancies of human nature.

The importance of Style is generally unsuspected by philosophers and men of science, who are quite aware of its advantage in all departments of BELLES LETTRES; and if you allude in their presence to the deplorably defective presentation of the ideas in some work distinguished for its learning, its profundity or its novelty, it is probable that you will be despised as a frivolous setter up of manner over matter, a light-minded DILLETANTE, unfitted for the simple austerities of science. But this is itself a light-minded contempt; a deeper insight would change the tone, and help to remove the disgraceful slovenliness and feebleness of composition which deface the majority of grave works, except those written by Frenchmen, who have been taught that composition is an art and that no writer may neglect it. In England and Germany, men who will spare no labour in research, grudge all labour in style; a morning is cheerfully devoted to verifying a quotation, by one who will not spare ten minutes to reconstruct a clumsy sentence; a reference is sought with ardour, an appropriate expression in lleu of the inexact phrase which first suggests itself does not seem worth seeking. What are we to say to a man who spends a quarter's income on a diamond pin which he sticks in a greasy cravat? A man who calls public attention on him, and appears in a slovenly undress? Am I to bestow applause on some insignificant parade of erudition, and withhold blame from the stupidities of style which surround it?

Had there been a clear understanding of Style as the living body of thought, and not its "dress," which might be more or less ornamental, the error I am noticing would not have spread so widely. But, naturally, when men regarded the grace of style as mere grace of manner, and not as the delicate precision giving form and relief to matter—as mere ornament, stuck on to arrest incurious eyes, and not as effective expression—their sense of the deeper value of matter made them despise such aid. A clearer conception would have rectified this error. The matter is confluent with the manner; and only THROUGH the style can thought reach the reader's mind. If the manner is involved, awkward, abrupt, obscure, the reader will either be oppressed with a confused sense of cumbrous material which awaits an artist to give it shape, or he will have the labour thrown upon him of extricating the material and reshaping it in his own mind.

How entirely men misconceive the relation of style to thought may be seen in the replies they make when their writing is objected to, or in the ludicrous attempts of clumsy playfulness and tawdry eloquence when they wish to be regarded as writers.

"Le style le moins noble a pourtant sa noblesse," and the principle of Sincerity, not less than the suggestions of taste, will preserve the integrity of each style. A philosopher, an investigator, an historian, or a moralist so far from being required to present the graces of a wit, an essayist, a pamphleteer, or a novelist, would be warned off such ground by the necessity of expressing himself sincerely. Pascal, Biot, Buffon, or Laplace are examples of the clearness and beauty with which ideas may be presented wearing all the graces of fine literature, and losing none of the severity of science. Bacon, also, having an opulent and active intellect, spontaneously expressed himself in forms of various excellence. But what a pitiable contrast is presented by Kant! It is true that Kant having a much narrower range of sensibility could have no such ample resource of expression, and he was wise in not attempting to rival the splendour of the NOVUM ORGANUM; but he was not simply unwise, he was extremely culpable in sending forth his thoughts as so much raw material which the public was invited to put into shape as it could. Had he been aware that much of his bad writing was imperfect thinking, and always imperfect adaptation of means to ends, he might have been induced to recast it into more logical and more intelligible sentences, which would have stimulated the reader's mind as much as they now oppress it. Nor had Kant the excuse of a subject too abstruse for clear presentation. The examples of Descartes, Spinoza, Hobbes, and Hume are enough to show how such subjects can be mastered, and the very implication of writing a book is that the writer has mastered his material and can give it intelligible form.

A grave treatise, dealing with a narrow range of subjects or moving amid severe abstractions, demands a gravity and severity of style which is dissimilar to that demanded by subjects of a wider scope or more impassioned impulse; but abstract philosophy has its appropriate elegance no less than mathematics. I do not mean that each subject should necessarily be confined to one special mode of treatment, in the sense which was understood when people spoke of the "dignity of history," and so forth. The style must express the writer's mind; and as variously constituted minds will treat one and the same subject, there will be varieties in their styles. If a severe thinker be also a man of wit, like Bacon, Hobbes, Pascal, or Galileo, the wit will flash its sudden illuminations on the argument; but if he be not a man of wit, and condescends to jest under the impression that by jesting he is giving an airy grace to his argument, we resent it as an impertinence.

I have throughout used Style in the narrower sense of expression rather than in the wider sense of "treatment" which is sometimes affixed to it. The mode of treating a subject is also no doubt the writer's or the artist's way of expressing what is in his mind, but this is Style in the more general sense, and does not admit of being reduced to laws apart from those of Vision and Sincerity. A man necessarily sees a subject in a particular light—ideal or grotesque, familiar or fanciful, tragic or humorous, he may wander into fairy-land, or move amid representative abstractions; he may follow his wayward fancy in its grotesque combinations, or he may settle down amid the homeliest details of daily life. But having chosen he must be true to his choice. He is not allowed to represent fairy-land as if it resembled Walworth, nor to paint Walworth in the colours of Venice. The truth of consistency must be preserved in his treatment, truth in art meaning of course only truth within the limits of the art; thus the painter may produce the utmost relief he can by means of light and shade, but is peremptorily forbidden to use actual solidities on a plane surface. He must represent gold by colour, not by sticking gold on his flgures. [This was done with naivete by the early painters, and is really very effective in the pictures of Gentile da Fabriano—that Paul Veronese of the fifteenth century—as the reader will confess if he has seen the "Adoration of the Magi," in the Florence Academy; but it could not be tolerated now]. Our applause is greatly determined by our sense of difficulty overcome, and to stick gold on a picture is an avoidance of the difficulty of painting it.

Truth of presentation has an inexplicable charm for us, and throws a halo round even ignoble objects. A policeman idly standing at the corner of the street, or a sow lazily sleeping against the sun, are not in nature objects to excite a thrill of delight, but a painter may, by the cunning of his art, represent them so as to delight every spectator. The same objects represented by an inferior painter will move only a languid interest; by a still more inferior painter they may be represented so as to please none but the most uncultivated eye. Each spectator is charmed in proportion to his recognition of a triumph over difficulty which is measured by the degree of verisimilitude. The degrees are many. In the lowest the pictured object is so remote from the reality that we simply recognise what the artist meant to represent. In like manner we recognise in poor novels and dramas what the authors mean to be characters, rather than what our experience of life suggests as characteristic.

Not only do we apportion our applause according to the degree of versimilitude attained, but also according to the difficulty each involves. It is a higher difficulty, and implies a nobler art to represent the movement and complexity of life and emotion than to catch the fixed lineaments of outward aspect. To paint a policeman idly lounging at the street corner with such verisimilitude that we are pleased with the representation, admiring the solidity of the figure, the texture of the clothes, and the human aspect of the features, is so difficult that we loudly applaud the skill which enables an artist to imitate what in itself is uninteresting; and if the imitation be carried to a certain degree of verisimilitude the picture may be of immense value. But no excellence of representation can make this high art. To carry it into the region of high art, another and far greater difficulty must be overcome; the man must be represented under the strain of great emotion, and we must recognise an equal truthfulness in the subtle indications of great mental agitation, the fleeting characters of which are far less easy to observe and to reproduce, than the stationary characters of form and costume. We may often observe how the novelist or dramatist has tolerable success so long as his personages are quiet, or moved only by the vulgar motives of ordinary life, and how fatally uninteresting, because unreal, these very personages become as soon as they are exhibited under the stress of emotion: their language ceases at once to be truthful, and becomes stagey; their conduct is no longer recognisable as that of human beings such as we have known. Here we note a defect of treatment, a mingling of styles, arising partly from defect of vision, and partly from an imperfect sincerity; and success in art will always be found dependent on integrity of style. The Dutch painters, so admirable in their own style, would become pitiable on quitting it for a higher.

But I need not enter at any length upon this subject of treatment. Obviously a work must have charm or it cannot succeed; and the charm will depend on very complex conditions in the artist's mind. What treatment is in Art, composition is in

Philosophy. The general conception of the point of view, and the skilful distribution of the masses, so as to secure the due preparation, development, and culmination, without wasteful prodigality or confusing want of symmetry, constitute Composition, which is to the structure of a treatise what Style—in the narrower sense—is to the structure of sentences. How far Style is reducible to law will be examined in the next chapter.

THE LAWS OF STYLE.

From what was said in the preceding chapter, the reader will understand that our present inquiry is only into the laws which regulate the mechanism of Style. In such an analysis all that constitutes the individuality, the life, the charm of a great writer, must escape. But we may dissect Style, as we dissect an organism, and lay bare the fundamental laws by which each is regulated. And this analogy may indicate the utility of our attempt; the grace and luminousness of a happy talent will no more be acquired by a knowledge of these laws, than the force and elasticity of a healthy organism will be given by a knowledge of anatomy; but the mistakes in Style, and the diseases of the organism, may be often avoided, and sometimes remedied, by such knowledge.

On a subject like this, which has for many years engaged the researches of many minds, I shall not be expected to bring forward discoveries; indeed, novelty would not unjustly be suspected of fallacy. The only claim my exposition can have on the reader's attention is that of being an attempt to systematise what has been hitherto either empirical observation, or the establishment of critical rules on a false basis. I know but of one exception to this sweeping censure, and that is the essay on the Philosophy of Style, by Mr. Herbert Spencer, [Spencer's ESSAYS: SCIENTIFIC, POLITICAL, AND SPECULATIVE. First Series. 1858]. where for the first time, I believe, the right method was pursued of seeking in psychological conditions for the true laws of expression.

The aims of Literature being instruction and delight, Style must in varying degrees appeal to our intellect and our sensibilities, sometimes reaching the intellect through the presentation of simple ideas, and at others through the agitating influence of emotions; sometimes awakening the sensibilities through the reflexes of ideas, and sometimes through a direct appeal. A truth may be nakedly expressed so as to stir the intellect alone; or it may be expressed in terms which, without disturbing its clearness, may appeal to our sensibility by their harmony or energy. It is not possible to distinguish the combined influences of clearness, movement, and harmony, so as to assign to each its relative effect; and if in the ensuing pages one law is isolated from another, this must be understood as an artifice inevitable in such investigations.

There are five laws under which all the conditions of Style may be grouped.—1. The Law of Economy. 2. The Law of Simplicity. 3. The Law of Sequence. 4, The Law of Climax. 5. The Law of Variety.

It would be easy to reduce these five to three, and range all considerations under Economy, Climax, and Variety; or we might amplify the divisions; but there are reasons of convenience as well as symmetry which give a preference to the five. I had arranged them thus for convenience some years ago, and I now find they express the equivalence of the two great factors of Style—-Intelligence and Sensibility. Two out of the five, Economy and Simplicity, more specially derive their significance from intellectual needs; another two, Climax and Variety, from emotional needs; and between these is the Law of Sequence, which is intermediate in its nature, and may be claimed with equal justice by both. The laws of force and the laws of pleasure can only be provisionally isolated in our inquiry; in style they are blended. The following brief estimate of each considers it as an isolated principle undetermined by any other.

1. THE LAW OF ECONOMY.

Our inquiry is scientific, not empirical; it therefore seeks the psychological basis for every law, endeavouring to ascertain what condition of a reader's receptivity determines the law. Fortunately for us, in the case of the first and most important law the psychological basis is extremely simple, and may be easily appreciated by a reference to its analogue in Mechanics.

What is the first object of a machine? Effective work—VIS VIVA. Every means by which friction can be reduced, and the force thus economised be rendered available, necessarily solicits the constructor's care. He seeks as far as possible to liberate the motion which is absorbed in the working of the machine, and to use it as VIS VIVA. He knows that every superfluous detail, every retarding influence, is at the cost of so much power, and is a mechanical defect though it may perhaps be an aesthetic beauty or a practical convenience. He may retain it because of the beauty, because of the convenience, but he knows the price of effective power at which it is obtained.

And thus it stands with Style. The first object of a writer is effective expression, the power of communicating distinct thoughts and emotional suggestions. He has to overcome the friction of ignorance and pre-occupation. He has to arrest a wandering attention, and to clear away the misconceptions which cling around verbal symbols. Words are not llke iron and wood, coal and water, invariable in their properties, calculable in their effects. They are mutable in their powers, deriving force and subtle variations of force from very trifling changes of position; colouring and coloured by the words which precede and succeed; significant or insignificant from the powers of rhythm and cadence. It is the writer's art so to arrange words that they shall suffer the least possible retardation from the inevitable friction of the reader's mind. The analogy of a machine is perfect. In both cases the object is to secure the maximum of disposable force, by diminishing the amount absorbed in the working. Obviously, if a reader is engaged in extricating the meaning from a sentence which ought to have reflected its meaning as in a mirror, the mental energy thus employed is abstracted from the amount of force which he has to bestow on the subject; he has mentally to form anew the sentence which has been clumsily formed by the writer; he wastes, on interpretation of the symbols, force which might have been concentrated on meditation of the propositions. This waste is inappreciable in writing of ordinary excellence, and on subjects not severely tasking to the attention; but if inappreciable, it is always waste; and in bad writing, especially on topics of philosophy and science, the waste is important. And it is this which greatly narrows the circle for serious works. Interest in the subjects treated of may not be wanting; but the abundant energy is wanting which to the fatigue of consecutive thinking will add the labour of deciphering the language. Many of us are but too familiar with the fatigue of reconstructing unwieldy sentences in which the clauses are not logically dependent, nor the terms free from equivoque; we know what it is to have to hunt for the meaning hidden in a maze of words; and we can understand the yawning indifference which must soon settle upon every reader of such writing, unless he has some strong external impulse or abundant energy.

Economy dictates that the meaning should be presented in a form which claims the least possible attention to itself as form, unless when that form is part of the writer's object, and when the simple thought is less important than the manner of presenting it. And even when the manner is playful or impassioned, the law of Economy still presides, and insists on the rejection of whatever is superfluous. Only a delicate susceptibility can discriminate a superfluity in passages of humour or rhetoric; but elsewhere a very ordinary understanding can recognise the clauses and the epithets which are out of place, and in excess, retarding or confusing the direct appreciation of the thought. If we have written a clumsy or confused sentence, we shall often find that the removal of an awkward inversion liberates the ides, or that the modification of a cadence increases the effect. This is sometimes strikingly seen at the rehearsal of a play: a passage which has fallen flat upon the ear is suddenly brightened into effectiveness by the removal of a superfluous phrase, which, by its retarding influence, had thwarted the declamatory crescendo.

Young writers may learn something of the secrets of Economy by careful revision of their own compositions, and by careful dissection of passages selected both from good and bad writers. They have simply to strike out every word, every clause, and every sentence, the removal of which will not carry away any of the constituent elements of the thought. Having done this, let them compare the revised with the unrevised passages, and see where the excision has improved, and where it has injured, the effect. For Economy, although a primal law, is not the only law of Style. It is subject to various limitations from the pressure of other laws; and thus the removal of a trifling superfluity will not be justified by a wise economy if that loss entails a dissonance, or prevents a climax, or robs the expression of its ease and variety. Economy is rejection of whatever is superfluous; it is not Miserliness. A liberal expenditure is often the best economy, and is always so when dictated by a generous impulse, not by a prodigal carelessness or ostentatious vanity. That man would greatly err who tried to make his style effective by stripping it of all redundancy and ornament, presenting it naked before the indifferent public. Perhaps the very redundancy which he lops away might have aided the reader to see the thought more clearly, because it would have kept the thought a little longer before his mind, and thus prevented him from hurrying on to the next while this one was still imperfectly conceived.

As a general rule, redundancy is injurious; and the reason of the rule will enable us to discriminate when redundancy is injurious and when beneficial. It is injurious when it hampers the rapid movement of the reader's mind, diverting his attention to some collateral detail. But it is beneficial when its retarding influence is such as only to detain the mind longer on the thought, and thus to secure the fuller effect of the thought. For rapid reading is often imperfect reading. The mind is satisfied with a glimpse of that which it ought to have steadily contemplated; and any artifice by which the thought can be kept long enough before the mind, may indeed be a redundancy as regards the meaning, but is an economy of power. Thus we see that the phrase or the clause which we might be tempted to lop away because it threw no light upon the proposition, would be retained by a skilful writer because it added power. You may know the character of a redundancy by this one test: does it divert the attention, or simply retard it? The former is always a loss of power; the latter is sometlmes a gain of power. The art of the writer consists in rejecting all redundancies that do not conduce to clearness. The shortest sentences are not necessarily the clearest. Concision gives energy, but it also adds restraint. The labour of expanding a terse sentence to its full meaning is often greater than the labour of picking out the meaning from a diffuse and loitering passage. Tacitus is more tiresome than Cicero.

There are occasions when the simplest and fewest words surpass in effect all the wealth of rhetorical amplification. An example may be seen in the passage which has been a favourite illustration from the days of Longinus to our own. "God said: Let there be light! and there was light." This is a conception of power so calm and simple that it needs only to be presented in the fewest and the plainest words, and would be confused or weakened by any suggestion of accessories. Let us amplify the expression in the redundant style of miscalled eloquent writers: "God, in the magnificent fulness of creative energy, exclaimed: Let there be light! and lo! the agitating fiat immediately went forth, and thus in one indivisible moment the whole universe was illumlned." We have here a sentence which I am certain many a writer would, in secret, prefer to the masterly plainness of Genesis. It is not a sentence which would have captivated critics.

Although this sentence from Genesis is sublime in its simplicity, we are not to conclude that simple sentences are uniformly the best, or that a style composed of propositions briefly expressed would obey a wise Economy. The reader's pleasure must not be forgotten; and he cannot be pleased by a style which always leaps and never flows. A harsh, abrupt, and dislocated manner irritates and perplexes him by its sudden jerks. It is easier to write short sentences than to read them. An easy, fluent, and harmonious phrase steals unobtrusively upon the mind, and allows the thought to expand quietly like an opening flower. But the very suasiveness of harmonious writing needs to be varied lest it become a drowsy monotony; and the sharp short sentences which are intolerable when abundant, when used sparingly act like a trumpet-call to the drooping attention.

II. THE LAW OF SIMPLICITY.

The first obligation of Economy is that of using the fewest words to secure the fullest effect. It rejects whatever is superfluous; but the question of superfluity must, as I showed just now, be determined in each individual case by various conditions too complex and numerous to be reduced within a formula. The same may be said of Simplicity, which is indeed so intimately allied with Economy that I have only given it a separate station for purposes of convenience. The psychological basis is the same for both. The desire for simplicity is impatience at superfluity, and the impatience arises from a sense of hindrance.

The first obligation of Simplicity is that of using the simplest means to secure the fullest effect. But although the mind instinctlvely rejects all needless complexity, we shall greatly err if we fail to recognise the fact, that what the mind recoils from is not the complexity, but the needlessness. When two men are set to the work of one, there is a waste of means; when two phrases are used to express one meaning twice, there is a waste of power; when incidents are multiplied and illustrations crowded without increase of illumination, there is prodigality which only the vulgar can mistake for opulence. Simplicity is a relative term. If in sketching the head of a man the artist wishes only to convey the general characteristics of that head, the fewest touches show the greatest power, selecting as they do only those details which carry with them characteristic significance. The means are simple, as the effect is simple. But if, besides the general characteristics, he wishes to convey the modelling of the forms, the play of light and shade, the textures, and the very complex effect of a human head, he must use more complex means. The simplicity which was adequate in the one case becomes totally inadequate in the other.

Obvious as this is, it has not been sufficiently present to the mind of critics who have called for plain, familiar, and concrete diction, as if that alone could claim to be simple; who have demanded a style unadorned by the artifices of involution, cadence, imagery, and epigram, as if Simplicity were incompatible with these; and have praised meagreness, mistaking it for Simplicity. Saxon words are words which in their homeliness have deep-seated power, and in some places they are the simplest because the most powerful words we can employ; but their very homeliness excludes them from certain places where their very power of suggestion is a disturbance of the general effect. The selective instinct of the artist tells him when his language should be homely, and when it should be more elevated; and it is precisely in the imperceptible blending of the plain with the ornate that a great writer is distinguished. He uses the simplest phrases without triviality, and the grandest without a suggestion of grandiloquence.

Simplicity of Style will therefore be understood as meaning absence of needless superfluity:

"Without o'erflowing full."

Its plainness is never meagreness, but unity. Obedient to the primary impulse of ADEQUATE expression, the style of a complex subject should be complex; of a technical subject, technical; of an abstract subject, abstract; of a familiar subject, familiar; of a pictorial subject, picturesque. The structure of the "Antigone" is simple; but so also is the structure of "Othello," though it contains many more elements; the simplicity of both lies in their fulness without superfluity.

Whatever is outside the purpose, or the feeling, of a scene, a speech, a sentence, or a phrase, whatever may be omitted without sacrifice of effect, is a sin against this law. I do not say that the incident, description, or dialogue, which may be omitted without injury to the unity of the work, is necessarily a sin against art; still less that, even when acknowledged as a sin, it may not sometimes be condoned by its success. The law of Simplicity is not the only law of art; and, moreover, audiences are, unhappily, so little accustomed to judge works as wholes, and so ready to seize upon any detail which pleases them, no matter how incongruously the detail may be placed, ["Was hilft's, wenn ihr ein Ganzes dargebracht! Das I'ublicum wird es euch doch zerpfiucken." —GOETHE]. That a felicitous fault will captivate applause, let critics shake reproving heads as they may. Nevertheless the law of Simplicity remains unshaken, and ought only to give way to the pressure of the law of Variety.

The drama offers a good opportunity for studying the operation of this law, because the limitations of time compel the dramatist to attend closely to what is and what is not needful for his purpose. A drama must compress into two or three hours material which may be diffused through three volumes of a novel, because spectators are more impatient than readers, and more unequivocally resent by their signs of weariness any disregard of economy, which in the novel may be skipped. The dramatist having little time in which to evolve his story, feels that every scene which does not forward the progress of the action or intensify the interest in the characters is an artistic defect; though in itself it may be charmingly written, and may excite applause, it is away from his immediate purpose. And what is true of purposeless scenes and characters which divert the current of progress, is equally true, in a minor degree, of speeches and sentences which arrest the culminating interest by calling attention away to other objects. It is an error which arises from a deficient earnestness on the writer's part, or from a too pliant facility. The DRAMATIS PERSONAE wander in their dialogue, not swayed by the fluctuations of feeling, but by the author's desire to show his wit and wisdom, or else by his want of power to control the vagrant suggestions of his fancy. The desire for display and the inability to control are weaknesses that lead to almost every transgression of Simplicity; but sometimes the transgressions are made in more or less conscious obedience to the law of Variety, although the highest reach of art is to secure variety by an opulent simplicity.

The novelist is not under the same limitations of time, nor has he to contend against the same mental impatience on the part of his public. He may therefore linger where the dramatist must hurry; he may digress, and gain fresh impetus from the digression, where the dramatist would seriously endanger the effect of his scene by retarding its evolution. The novelist with a prudent prodigality may employ descriptions, dialogues, and episodes, which would be fatal in a drama. Characters may be introduced and dismissed without having any important connection with the plot; it is enough if they serve the purpose of the chapter in which they appear. Although as a matter of fine art no character should have a place in a novel unless it form an integral element of the story, and no episode should be introduced unless it reflects some strong light on the characters or incidents, this is a critical demand which only fine artists think of satisfying, and only delicate tastes appreciate. For the mass of readers it is enough if they are mused; and indeed all readers, no matter how critical their taste, would rather be pleased by a transgression of the law than wearied by prescription. Delight condones offence. The only question for the writer is, whether the offence is so trivial as to be submerged in the delight. And he will do well to remember that the greater flexibility belonging to the novel by no means removes the novel from the laws which rule the drama. The parts of a novel should have organic relations. Push the licence to excess, and stitch together a volume of unrelated chapters,—a patchwork of descriptions, dialogues, and incidents,—no one will call that a novel; and the less the work has of this unorganised character the greater will be its value, not only in the eyes of critics, but in its effect on the emotions of the reader.

Simplicity of structure means organic unity, whether the organism be simple or complex; and hence in all times the emphasis which critics have laid upon Simplicity, though they have not unfrequently confounded it with narrowness of range. In like manner, as we said just now, when treating of diction they have overlooked the fact that the simplest must be that which best expresses the thought. Simplicity of diction is integrity of speech; that which admits of least equivocation, that which by the clearest verbal symbols most readily calls up in the reader's mind the images and feelings which the writer wishes to call up. Such diction may be concrete or abstract, familiar or technical; its simplicity is determined by the nature of the thought. We shall often be simpler in using abstract and technical terms than in using concrete and familiar terms which by their very concreteness and familiarity call up images and feelings foreign to our immediate purpose. If we desire the attention to fall upon some general idea we only blur its outlines by using words that call up particulars. Thus, although it may be needful to give some definite direction to the reader's thoughts by the suggestion of a particular fact, we must be careful not to arrest his attention on the fact itself, still less to divert it by calling up vivid images of facts unrelated to our present purpose. For example, I wish to fix in the reader's mind a conception of a lonely meditative man walking on the sea-shore, and I fall into the vicious style of our day which is lauded as word-painting, and write something like this :—

"The fishermen mending their storm-beaten boats upon the shore would lay down the hammer to gaze after him as he passed abstractedly before their huts, his hair streaming in the salt breeze, his feet crushing the scattered seaweed, his eyes dreamily fixed upon the purple heights of the precipitous crags."

Now it is obvious that the details here assembled are mostly foreign to my purpose, which has nothing whatever to do with fishermen, storms, boats, sea-weeds, or purple crags; and by calling up images of these I only divert the attention from my thought. Whereas, if it had been my purpose to picture the scene itself, or the man's delight in it, then the enumeration of details would give colour and distinctness to the picture.

The art of a great writer is seen in the perfect fitness of his expressions. He knows how to blend vividness with vagueness, knows where images are needed, and where by their vivacity they would be obstacles to the rapid appreciation of his thought. The value of concrete illustration artfully used may be seen illustrated in a passage from Macaulay's invective against Frederick the Great: "On his head is all the blood which was shod in a war which raged during many years and in every quarter of the globe, the blood of the column at Fentonoy, the blood of the mountaineers who were slaughtered at Culloden. The evils produced by his wickedness were felt in lands where the name of Prussia was unknown; and in order that he might rob a neighbour whom he had promised to defend, black men fought on the coast of Coromandel and red men scalped each other by the great lakes of North America." Disregarding the justice or injustice of the thought, note the singular force and beauty of this passage, delightful alike to ear and mind; and observe how its very elaborateness has the effect of the finest simplicity, because the successive pictures are constituents of the general thought, and by their vividness render the conclusion more impressive. Let us suppose him to have wrltten with the vague generality of expression much patronised by dignified historians, and told us that "Frederick was the cause of great European conflicts extending over long periods; and in consequence of his political aggression hideous crimes were perpetrated in the most distant parts of the globe." This absence of concrete images would not have been simplicity, inasmuch as the labour of converting the general expressions into definite meanings would thus have been thrown upon the reader.

Pictorial illustration has its dangers, as we daily see in the clumsy imitators of Macaulay, who have not the fine instinct of style, but obey the vulgar instinct of display, and imagine they can produce a brilliant effect by the use of strong lights, whereas they distract the attention with images alien to the general impression, just as crude colourists vex the eye with importunate splendours. Nay, even good writers sometimes sacrifice the large effect of a diffusive light to the small effect of a brilliant point. This is a defect of taste frequently noticeable in two very good writers, De Quincey and Ruskin, whose command of expression is so varied that it tempts them into FIORITURA as flexibility of voice tempts singers to sin against simplicity. At the close of an eloquent passage De Quincey writes :—

"Gravitation that works without holiday for ever and searches every corner of the universe, what intellect can follow it to its fountains? And yet, shyer than gravitation, less to be counted on than the fluxions of sun-dials, stealthier than the growth of a forest, are the footsteps of Christianity amongst the political workings of man."

The association of holidays and shyness with an idea so abstract as that of gravitation, the use of the learned word fluxions to express the movements of the shadows on a dial, and the discordant suggestion of stealthiness applied to vegetable growth and Christianity, are so many offences against simplicity. Let the passage be contrasted with one in which wealth of imagery is in accordance with the thought it expresses:—

"In the edifices of man there should be found reverent worship and following, not only of the spirit which rounds the pillars of the forest, and arches the vault of the avenue—which gives veining to the leaf and polish to the shell, and grace to every pulse that agitates animal organisation but of that also which reproves the pillars of the earth, and builds up her barren precipices into the coldness of the clouds, and lifts her shadowy cones of mountain purple into the pale arch of the sky; for these and other glories more than these refuse not to connect themselves in his thoughts with the work of his own hand; the grey cliff loses not its nobleness when it reminds us of some

Cyclopoan waste of mural stone; the pinnacles of the rocky promontory arrange themselves, undegraded, into fantastic semblances of fortress towns; and even the awful cone of the far-off mountain has a melancholy mixed with that of its own solitude, which is cast from the images of nameless tumuli on white sea-shores, and of the heaps of reedy clay into which chambered cities melt in their mortality." [Ruskin].

I shall notice but two points in this singularly beautiful passage. The one is the exquisite instinct of Sequence in several of the phrases, not only as to harmony, but as to the evolution of the meaning, especially in "builds up her barren precipices into the coldness of the clouds, and lifts her shadowy cones of mountain purple into the pale arch of the sky." The other is the injurious effect of three words in the sentence, "for these and other glories more than these REFUSE NOT TO connect themselves in his thoughts." Strike out the words printed in italics, and you not only improve the harmony, but free the sentence from a disturbing use of what Ruskin has named the "pathetic fallacy." There are times in which Nature may be assumed as in sympathy with our moods; and at such times the pathetic fallacy is a source of subtle effect. But in the passage just quoted the introduction seems to me a mistake: the simplicity of the thought is disturbed by this hint of an active participation of Nature in man's feelings; it is preserved in its integrity by the omission of that hint.

These illustrations will suffice to show how the law we are considering will command and forbid the use of concrete expressions and vivid imagery according to the purpose of the writer. A fine taste guided by Sincerity will determine that use. Nothing more than a general rule can be laid down. Eloquence, as I said before, cannot spring from the simple desire to be eloquent; the desire usually leads to grandiloquence. But Sincerity will save us. We have but to remember Montesquieu's advice: "Il faut prendre garde aux grandes phrases dans les humbles sujets; elles produisent l'effet d'une masque a barbe blanche sur la joue d'un enfant."

Here another warning may be placed. In our anxiety lest we err on the side of grandiloquence we may perhaps fall into the opposite error of tameness. Sincerity will save us here also. Let us but express the thought and feeling actually in our minds, then our very grandiloquence (if that is our weakness) will have a certain movement and vivacity not without effect, and our tameness (if we are tame) will have a gentleness not without its charm.

Finally, let us banish from our critical superstitions the notion that chastity of composition, or simplicity of Style, is in any respect allied to timidity. There are two kinds of timidity, or rather it has two different origins, both of which cripple the free movement of thought. The one is the timidity of fastidiousness, the other of placid stupidity: the one shrinks from originality lest it should be regarded as impertinent; the other lest, being new, it should be wrong. We detect the one in the sensitive discreetness of the style. We detect the other in the complacency of its platitudes and the stereotyped commonness of its metaphors. The writer who is afraid of originality feels himself in deep water when he launches into a commonplace. For him who is timid because weak, there is no advice, except suggesting the propriety of silence. For him who is timid because fastidious, there is this advice: get rid of the superstition about chastity, and recognise the truth that a style may be simple, even if it move amid abstractions, or employ few Saxon words, or abound in concrete images and novel turns of expression.

III. THE LAW OF SEQUENCE.

Much that might be included under this head would equally well find its place under that of Economy or that of Climax.

Indeed it is obvious that to secure perfect Economy there must be that sequence of the words which will present the least obstacle to the unfolding of the thought, and that Climax is only attainable through a properly graduated sequence. But there is another element we have to take into account, and that is the rhythmical effect of Style. Mr. Herbert Spencer in his Essay very clearly states the law of Sequence, but I infer that he would include it entirely under the law of Economy; at any rate he treats of it solely in reference to intelligibility, and not at all in its scarcely less important relation to harmony. We have A PRIORI reasons," he says, "for believing that in every sentence there is one order of words more effective than any other, and that this order is the one which presents the elements of the proposition in the succession in which they may be most readily put together. As in a narrative, the events should be stated in such sequence that the mind may not have to go backwards and forwards in order rightly to connect them; as in a group of sentences, the arrangement should be such that each of them may be understood as it comes, without waiting for the subsequent ones; so in every sentence, the sequence of the words should be that which suggests the constituents of the thought in the order most convenient for building up that thought."

But Style appeals to the emotions as well as to the intellect, and the arrangement of words and sentences which will be the most economical may not be the most musical, and the most musical may not be the most pleasurably effective. For Climax and Variety it may be necessary to sacrifice something of rapid intelligibillty: hence involutions, antitheses, and suspensions, which disturb the most orderly arrangement, may yet, in virtue of their own subtle influences, be counted as improvements on that arrangement.

Tested by the Intellect and the Feelings, the law of Sequence is seen to be a curious compound of the two. If we isolate these elements for the purposes of exposition, we shall find that the principle of the first is much simpler and more easy of obedience than the principle of the second. It may be thus stated: —

The constituent elements of the conception expressed in the sentence and the paragraph should be arranged in strict correspondence with an inductive or a deductive progression.

All exposition, like all research, is either inductive or deductive. It groups particulars so as to lead up to a general conception which embraces them all, but which could not be fully understood until they had been estimated; or else it starts from some general conception, already familar to the mind, and as it moves along, casts its light upon numerous particulars, which are thus shown to be related to it, but which without that light would have been overlooked.

If the reader will meditate on that brief statement of the principle, he will, I think, find it explain many doubtful points. Let me merely notice one, namely, the dispute as to whether the direct or the indirect style should be preferred. Some writers insist, and others practise the precept without insistance, that the proposition should be stated first, and all its qualifications as well as its evidences be made to follow; others maintain that the proposition should be made to grow up step by step with all its evidences and qualifications in their due order, and the conclusion disclose itself as crowning the whole. Are not both methods right under different circumstances? If my object is to convince you of a general truth, or to impress you with a feeling, which you are not already prepared to accept, it is obvious that the most effective method is the inductive, which leads your mind upon a culminating wave of evidence or emotion to the very point I aim at. But the deductive method is best when I wish to direct the light of familiar truths and roused emotions, upon new particulars, or upon details in unsuspected relation to those truths; and when I wish the attention to be absorbed by these particulars which are of interest in themselves, not upon the general truths which are of no present interest except in as far as they light up these details. A growing thought requires the inductive exposition, an applied thought the deductive.

This principle, which is of very wide application, is subject to two important qualifications—one pressed on it by the necessities of Climax and Variety, the other by the feebleness of memory, which cannot keep a long hold of details unless their significance is apprehended; so that a paragraph of suspended meaning should never be long, and when the necessities of the case bring together numerous particulars in evidence of the conclusion, they should be so arranged as to have culminating force: one clause leading up to another, and throwing its impetus into it, instead of being linked on to another, and dragging the mind down with its weight.

It is surprising how few men understand that Style is a Fine Art; and how few of those who are fastidious in their diction give much care to the arrangement of their sentences, paragraphs, and chapters—in a word, to Composition. The painter distributes his masses with a view to general effect; so does the musician: writers seldom do so. Nor do they usually arrange the members of their sentences in that sequence which shall secure for each its proper emphasis and its determining influence on the others—influence reflected back and influence projected forward. As an example of the charm that lies in unostentatious antiphony, consider this passage from Ruskin:—"Originality in expression does not depend on invention of new words; nor originality in poetry on invention of new measures; nor in painting on invention of new colours or new modes of using them. The chords of music, the harmonies of colour, the general principles of the arrangement of sculptural masses, have been determined long ago, and in all probability cannot be added to any more than they can be altered." Men write like this by instinct; and I by no means wish to suggest that writing like this can be produced by rule. What I suggest is, that in this, as in every other Fine Art, instinct does mostly find itself in accordance with rule; and a knowledge of rules helps to direct the blind gropings of feeling, and to correct the occasional mistakes of instinct. If, after working his way through a long and involved sentence in which the meaning is rough hewn, the writer were to try its effect upon ear and intellect, he might see its defects and re-shape it into beauty and clearness. But in general men shirk this labour, partly because it is irksome, and partly because they have no distinct conception of the rules which would make the labour light.

The law of Sequence, we have seen, rests upon the two requisites of Clearness and Harmony. Men with a delicate sense of rhythm will instinctively distribute their phrases in an order that falls agreeably on the ear, without monotony, and without an echo of other voices; and men with a keen sense of logical relation will instinctively arrange their sentences in an order that best unfolds the meaning. The French are great masters of the law of Sequence, and, did space Permit, I could cite many excellent examples. One brief passage from Royer Collard must suffice:—"Les faits que l'observation laisse epars et muets la causalite les rassemble, les enchaine, leur prete un langage. Chaque fait revele celui qui a precede, prophetise celui qui va suivre."

The ear is only a guide to the harmony of a Period, and often tempts us into the feebleness of expletives or approximative expressions for the sake of a cadence. Yet, on the other hand, if we disregard the subtle influences of harmonious arrangement, our thoughts lose much of the force which would otherwise result from their logical subordination. The easy evolution of thought in a melodious period, quietly taking up on its way a variety of incidental details, yet never lingering long enough over them to divert the attention or to suspend the continuous crescendo of interest, but by subtle influences of proportion allowing each clause of the sentence its separate significance, is the product of a natural gift, as rare as the gift of music, or of poetry. But until men come to understand that Style is an art, and an amazingly difficult art, they will continue with careless presumption to tumble out their sentences as they would lilt stones from a cart, trusting very much to accident or gravitation for the shapeliness of the result. I will write a passage which may serve as an example of what I mean, although the defect is purposely kept within very ordinary limlts—

"To construct a sentence with many loosely and not obviously dependent clauses, each clause containing an important meaning or a concrete image the vivacity of which, like a boulder in a shallow stream, disturbs the equable current of thought, and in such a case the more beautiful the image the greater the obstacle, so that the laws of simplicity and economy are violated by it,—while each clause really requires for its interpretation a proposition that is however kept suspended till the close, is a defect."

The weariness produced by such writing as this is very great, and yet the recasting of the passage is easy. Thus:—

"It is a defect when a sentence is constructed with many loosely and not obviously dependent clauses, each of which requires for its interpretation a preposition that is kept suspended till the close; and this defect is exaggerated when each clause contains an important meaning, or a concrete image which, like a boulder in a shallow stream, disturbs the equable current of thought: the more beautiful the image, the greater its violation of the laws of simplicity and economy."

In this second form the sentence has no long suspension of the main idea, no diversions of the current. The proposition is stated and illustrated directly, and the mind of the reader follows that of the writer. How injurious it is to keep the key in your pocket until all the locks in succession have been displayed may be seen in such a sentence as this:—

"Phantoms of lost power, sudden intuitions and shadowy restorations of forgotten feelings, sometimes dim and perplexing, sometimes by bright but furtive glimpses, sometimes by a full and steady revelation overcharged with light, throw us back in a moment upon scenes and remembrances that we have left full thirty years behind us."

Had De Quincey liberated our minds from suspense by first presenting the thought which first arose in his own mind,—namely, that we are thrown back upon scenes and remembrances by phantoms of lost power, &c.—the beauty of his language in its pregnant suggestiveness would have been felt at once. Instead of that, he makes us accompany him in darkness, and when the light appears we have to travel backwards over the ground again to see what we have passed. The passage continues:—

"In solitudes, and chiefly in the solitudes of nature, and, above all, amongst the great and enduring features of nature, such as mountains and quiet dells, and the lawny recesses of forests, and the silent shores of lakes—features with which (as being themselves less liable to change) our feelings have a more abiding associatlon,—under these circumstances it is that such evanescent hauntings of our forgotten selves are most apt to startle and waylay us."

The beauty of this passage seems to me marred by the awkward yet necessary interruption, "under these circumstances it is," which would have been avoided by opening the sentence with "such evanescent hauntings of our forgotten selves are most apt to startle us in solitudes," &c. Compare the effect of directness in the following:—

"This was one of the most common shapes of extinguished power from which Coleridge fled to the great city. But sometimes the same decay came back upon his heart in the more poignant shape of intimations and vanishing glimpses recovered for one moment from the Paradise of youth, and from fields of joy and power, over which for him too certainly he felt that the cloud of night was settling for ever."

Obedience to the law of Sequence gives strength by giving clearness and beauty of rhythm; it economises force and creates music. A very trifling disregard of it will mar an effect. See an example both of obedience and trifling disobedience in the following passage from Ruskin: –

"People speak in this working age, when they speak from their hearts, as if houses and lands and food and raiment were alone useful, and as if Sight, Thought, and Admiration were all profitless, so that men insolently call themselves Utilitarians, who would turn, if they had their way, themselves and their race into vegetables; men who think, as far as such can be said to think, that the meat is more than life and the raiment than the body, who look on earth as a stable and to its fruit as fodder; vinedressers and husbandmen who love the corn they grind and the grapes they crush better than the gardens of the angels upon the slopes of Eden."

It is instinctive to contrast the dislocated sentence, "who would turn, if they had their way, themselves and their race," with the sentence which succeeds it, "men who think, as far as such men can be said to think, that the meat," &c. In the latter the parenthetic interruption is a source of power: it dams the current to increase its force; in the former the inversion is a loss of power: it is a dissonance to the ear and a diversion of the thought.

As illustrations of Sequence in composition, two passages may be quoted from Macaulay which display the power of pictorial suggestions when, instead of diverting attention from the main purpose, they are arranged with progressive and culminating effect.

"Such, or nearly such, was the change which passed on the Mogul empire during the forty years which followed the death of Aurungzebe. A series of nominal sovereigns, sunk in indolence and debauchery, sauntered away life in secluded palaces, chewing bang, fondling dancing girls, and listening to buffoons. A series of ferocious invaders had descended through the western passes to prey on the defenceless wealth of Hindostan. A Persian conqueror crossed the Indus, marched through the gates of Delhi, and bore away in triumph those treasures of which the magnificence had astounded Roe and Bernier;—the peacock throne, on which the richest jewels of Golconda had been disposed by the most skilful hands of Europe, and the inestimable Mountain of Light, which, after many strange vicissitudes, lately shone in the bracelet of Runjeet Sing, and is now destined to adorn the hideous idol of Prista. The Afghan soon followed to complete the work of devastation which the Persian had begun. The warlike tribe of Rajpoots threw off the Mussulman yoke. A band of'mercenary soldiers occupied the Rohilcund. The Seiks ruled on the Indus. The Jauts spread terror along the Jumnah. The high lands which border on the western sea-coast of India poured forth a yet more formidable race—a race which was long the terror of every native power, and which yielded only after many desperate and doubtful struggles to the fortune and genius of England. It was under the reign of Aurungzebe that this wild clan of plunderers first descended from the mountains; and soon after his death every corner of his wide empire learned to tremble at the mighty name of the Mahrattas. Many fertile viceroyalties were entirely subdued by them. Their dominions stretched across the peninsula from sea to sea. Their captains reigned at Poonah, at Gualior, in Guzerat, in Berar, and in Tanjore."

Such prose as this affects us like poetry. The pictures and suggestions might possibly have been gathered together by any other historian; but the artful succession, the perfect sequence, could only have been found by a fine writer. I pass over a few paragraphs, and pause at this second example of a sentence simple in structure, though complex in its elements, fed but not overfed with material, and almost perfect in its cadence and logical connection. "Scarcely any man, however sagacious, would have thought it possible that a trading company, separated from India by fifteen thousand miles of sea, and possessing in India only a few acres for purposes of commerce, would in less than a hundred years spread its empire from Cape Comorin to the eternal snows of the Himalayas—would compel Mahratta and Mahomedan to forget their mutual feuds in common subjection—would tame down even those wild races which had resisted the most powerful of the Moguls; and having established a government far stronger than any ever known in those countries, would carry its victorious arms far to the east of the Burrampooter, and far to the west of the Hydaspes—dictate terms of peace at the gates of Ava, and seat its vassals on the throne of Candahar."

Let us see the same principle exhibited in a passage at once pictorial and argumentative. "We know more certainly every day," says Ruskin, "that whatever appears to us harmful in the universe has some beneficent or necessary operation; that the storm which destroys a harvest brightens the sunbeams for harvests yet unsown, and that a volcano which buries a city preserves a thousand from destruction. But the evil is not for the time less fearful because we have learned it to be necessary; and we can easily understand the timidity or the tenderness of the spirit which could withdraw itself from the presence of destruction, and create in its imagination a world of which the peace should be unbroken, in which the sky should not darken nor the sea rage, in which the leaf should not change nor the blossom wither. That man is greater, however, who contemplates with an equal mind the alternations of terror and of beauty; who, not rejoicing less beneath the sunny sky, can also bear to watch the bars of twilight narrowing on the horizon; and, not less sensible to the blessing of the peace of nature, can rejoice in the magnificence of the ordinances by which that peace is protected and secured. But separated from both by an immeasurable distance would be the man who delighted in convulsion and disease for their own sake; who found his daily food in the disorder of nature mingled with the suffering of humanity; and watched joyfully at the right hand of the Angel whose appointed work is to destroy as well as to accuse, while the corners of the house of feasting were struck by the wind from the wilderness."

I will now cite a passage from Burke, which will seem tame after the pictorial animation of the passages from Macaulay and Ruskin; but which, because it is simply an exposition of opinions addressed to the understanding, will excellently illustrate the principle I am enforcing. He is treating of the dethronement of kings. "As it was not made for common abuses, so it is not to be agitated by common minds. The speculative line of demarcation, where obedience ought to end and resistance must begin, is faint, obscure, and not easily definable. It is not a single act or a single event which determines it. Governments must be abused and deranged, indeed, before it can be thought of; and the prospect of the future must be as bad as the experience of the past. When things are in that lamentable condition, the nature of the disease is to indicate the remedy to those whom nature has qualified to administer in extremities this critical, ambiguous, bitter potion to a distempered state. Times and occasions and provocations will teach their own lessons. The wise will determine from the gravity of the case; the irritable from sensibility to oppression; the high-minded from disdain and indignation at abusive power in unworthy hands; the brave and bold from love of honourable danger in a generous cause. But with or without right, a revolution will be the very last resource of the thinking and the good."

As a final example I will cite a passage from M. Taine: —"De la encore cette insolence contre les inferieurs, et ce mepris verse d'etage en etage depuis le premier jusqu'au dernier. Lorsque dans une societe la loi consacre les conditions inegales, personne n'est exempt d'insulte; le grand seigneur, outrage par le roi, outrage le noble qui outrage le peuple; la nature humaine est humilie a tous les etages, et la societe n'est plus qu'un commerce d'affronts."

The law of Sequence by no means prescribes that we should invariably state the proposition before its qualifications—the thought before its illustrations; it merely prescribes that we should arrange our phrases in the order of logical dependence and rhythmical cadence, the order best suited for clearness and for harmony. The nature of the thought will determine the one, our sense of euphony the other.

IV. THE LAW OF CLIMAX.

We need not pause long over this; it is generally understood. The condition of our sensibilities is such that to produce their effect stimulants must be progressive in intensity and varied in kind. On this condition rest the laws of Climax and Variety. The phrase or image which in one position will have a mild power of occupying the thoughts, or stimulating the emotions, loses this power if made to succeed one of like kind but more agitating influence, and will gain an accession of power if it be artfully placed on the wave of a climax. We laugh at "then came Dalhousie, that great God of War, Lieutenant-Colonel to the Earl of Mar," because of the relaxation which follows the sudden tension of the mind; but if we remove the idea of the colonelcy from this position of anti-climax, the same couplet becomes energetic rather than ludicrous—"Lieutenant-Colonel to the Earl of Mar, then came Dalhousie, that great God of War."

I have selected this strongly marked case, instead of several feeble passages which might be chosen from the first book at hand, wherein carelessness allows the sentences to close with the least important, phrases, and the style droops under frequent anti-climax. Let me now cite a passage from Macaulay which vividly illustrates the effect of Climax:—

"Never, perhaps, was the change which the progress of civilisation has produced in the art of war more strikingly illustrated than on that day. Ajax beating down the Trojan leader with a rock which two ordinary men could scarcely lift; Horatius defending the bridge against an army; Richard, the lion-hearted, spurring along the whole Saracen line without finding an enemy to withstand his assault; Robert Bruce crushing with one blow the helmet and head of Sir Harry Bohun in sight of the whole array of England and Scotland,—such are the heroes of a dark age. [Here is an example of suspended meaning, where the suspense intensifies the effect, because each particular is vividly apprehended in itself, and all culminate in the conclusion; they do not complicate the thought, or puzzle us, they only heighten expectation]. In such an age bodily vigour is the most indispensable qualification of a warrior. At Landen two poor sickly beings, who, in a rude state of society, would have been regarded as too puny to bear any part in combats, were the souls of two great armies. In some heathen countries they would have been exposed while infants. In Christendom they would, six hundred years earlier, have been sent to some quiet cloister. But their lot had fallen on a time when men had discovered that the strength of the muscles is far inferior in value to the strength of the mind. It is probable that among the hundred and twenty thousand soldiers that were marshalled round Neerwinden, under all the standards of Western Europe, the two feeblest in body were the hunchbacked dwarf, who urged forward the fiery onset of France, and the asthmatic skeleton who covered the slow retreat of England."

The effect of Climax is very marked in the drama. Every speech, every scene, every act, should have its progressive sequence. Nothing can be more injudicious than a trivial phrase following an energetic phrase, a feeble thought succeeding a burst of passion, or even a passionate thought succeeding one more passionate. Yet this error is frequently committed.

In the drama all laws of Style are more imperious than in fiction or prose of any kind, because the art is more intense. But Climax is demanded in every species of composition, for it springs from a psychological necessity. It is pressed upon, however, by the law of Variety in a way to make it far from safe to be too rigidly followed. It easily degenerates into monotony.

V. THE LAW OF VARIETY.

Some one, after detailing an elaborate recipe for a salad, wound up the enumeration of ingredients and quantities with the advice to "open the window and throw it all away." This advice might be applied to the foregoing enumeration of the laws of Style, unless these were supplemented by the important law of Variety. A style which rigidly interpreted the precepts of economy, simplicity, sequence, and climax, which rejected all superfluous words and redundant ornaments, adopted the easiest and most logical arrangement, and closed every sentence and every paragraph with a climax, might be a very perfect bit of mosaic, but would want the glow and movement of a living mind. Monotony would settle on it like a paralysing frost. A series of sentences in which every phrase was a distinct thought, would no more serve as pabulum for the mind, than portable soup freed from all the fibrous tissues of meat and vegetable would serve as food for the body. Animals perish from hunger in the presence of pure albumen; and minds would lapse into idiocy in the presence of unadulterated thought. But without invoking extreme cases, let us simply remember the psychological fact that it is as easy for sentences to be too compact as for food to be too concentrated; and that many a happy negligence, which to microscopic criticism may appear defective, will be the means of giving clearness and grace to a style. Of course the indolent indulgence in this laxity robs style of all grace and power. But monotony in the structure of sentences, monotony of cadence, monotony of climax, monotony anywhere, necessarily defeats the very aim and end of style; it calls attention to the manner; it blunts the sensibilities; it renders excellences odious.

"Beauty deprived of its proper foils and adjuncts ceases to be enjoyed as beauty, just as light deprived of all shadow ceases to be enjoyed as light. A white canvas cannot produce an effect of sunshine; the painter must darken it in some places before he can make it look luminous in others; nor can the uninterrupted succession of beauty produce the true effect of beauty; it must be foiled by inferiority before its own power can be developed. Nature has for the most part mingled her inferior and noble elements as she mingles sunshine with shade, giving due influence to both. The truly high and beautiful art of Angelico is continually refreshed and strengthened by his frank portraiture of the most ordinary features of his brother monks, of the recorded peculiarities of ungainly sanctity; but the modern German and Raphaelesque schools lose all honour and nobleness in barber-like admiration of handsome faces, and have in fact no real faith except in straight noses and curled hair. Paul Veronese opposes the dwarf to the soldier, and the negress to the queen; Shakspeare places Caliban beside Miranda, and Autolycus beside Perdita; but the vulgar idealist withdraws his beauty to the safety of the saloon, and his innocence to the seclusion of the cloister; he pretends that he does this in delicacy of choice and purity of sentiment, while in truth he has neither courage to front the monster nor wit enough to furnish the knave." [Ruskin].

And how is Variety to be secured? The plan is simple, but like many other simple plans, is not without difficulty. It is for the writer to obey the great cardinal principle of Sincerity, and be brave enough to express himself in his own way, following the mood of his own mind, rather than endeavouring to catch the accents of another, or to adapt himself to some standard of taste. No man really thinks and feels monotonously. If he is monotonous in his manner of setting forth his thoughts and feelings, that is either because he has not learned the art of writing, or because he is more or less consciously imitating the manner of others. The subtle play of thought will give movement and life to his style if he do not clog it with critical superstitions. I do not say that it will give him grace and power; I do not say that relying on perfect sincerity will make him a fine writer, because sincerity will not give talent; but I say that sincerity will give him all the power that is possible to him, and will secure him the inestimable excellence of Variety.

❋❋❋❋❋